What Life Was Like®

IN EUROPE'S ROMANTIC ERA

Europe

AD 1789 ~ 1848

What Life Was Like

IN EUROPE'S ROMANTIC ERA

Europe
AD 1789 – 1848

BY THE EDITORS OF TIME-LIFE BOOKS, ALEXANDRIA, VIRGINIA

CONTENTS

In Europe's
Romantic Era

Revolutions and Romanticism

The fall of the Bastille—the Paris prison and symbol of royal tyranny—on July 14, 1789, heralded the beginning of the French Revolution. But the most important act of the revolutionaries occurred the following month: the drafting of the Declaration of the Rights of Man and of the Citizen. This document, which spelled out the basic human rights—the rights of speech, press, assembly, religion, and property and the equality of all people before the law—transmitted the ideas of the Revolution to the rest of Europe.

Much of Europe was stirred by the revolutionaries' ideals of liberty and equality. But the ensuing bloody Reign of Terror horrified many champions of the cause, and the execution of France's rightful king and queen left other European leaders feeling threatened. As a result, France had to fight a number of costly wars against Austria, Prussia, Spain, and Britain.

In these uncertain times, French military officer Napoleon Bonaparte captured the hearts both of his countrymen and of many other Europeans eager for a hero. When Napoleon crowned himself emperor in 1804, however, his disillusioned followers branded him a traitor to the Revolution. Over the next few years, his military campaigns, which brought more and more territory under French control, incited anger and apprehension throughout Europe. In 1814, an allied European force invaded France and forced Napoleon to abdicate. He again seized power briefly the following year but was again defeated.

At the Congress of Vienna, European leaders sought to restore order in the land. In France, allied leaders had already enthroned a new Bourbon king,

1789	1792	1793	1795	1796	1792-1802
The French Revolution begins; the Estates-General reconstitutes itself as the National Assembly; Parisians storm the Bastille	France is proclaimed a republic; Mary Wollstonecraft publishes *Vindication of the Rights of Woman*	The Reign of Terror begins under the direction of Maximilien Robespierre; Louis XVI is beheaded	The Directory—a legislative body and five-man executive council—assumes power in France	English physician Edward Jenner pioneers a vaccination for smallpox	France wars with Austria, Prussia, Spain, and Great Britain

Louis XVIII, who had agreed to relinquish all territories won by France since 1792. The German states—having dissolved the Confederation of the Rhine established and controlled by Napoleon—formed the German Confederation, which left most authority in the hands of the individual rulers. With these and other political moves, the congress hoped to return Europe to its old balance of power.

Instead, the revolution in France set off revolts in other parts of the continent. An uprising against the Dutch-led Kingdom of the Netherlands resulted in the independence of Belgium. Elsewhere, the Austrian government brutally suppressed an uprising in its northern Italian territory, while an insurrection in Poland left that country firmly under Russian control. Britain, meanwhile, dealt with growing discontent among its rising middle class by passing a reform act that provided them with more equitable representation in Parliament and gave many more the right to vote.

In Britain, another type of revolution had helped create this new middle class—the Industrial Revolution, begun not with the force of arms but with steam power. Within 20 years of the patent of James Watt's steam engine in 1769, steam was powering British forges, pumps, looms, carriages, and ships. By 1814 steam-powered printing presses enabled more widespread dissemination of news, and by 1830 steam-powered trains and London buses were common sights. The first industry to be revolutionized was cotton manufacturing. Mechanical advances in mining, metallurgy, and other industries followed, leading to still more economic growth. Distant markets were established and goods flowed between continents, sped overseas by new steamships.

Although the growing middle class prospered with these innovations, many in the lower classes did not. To support themselves, poor men, women, and children—many of them rural laborers forced off the land by improvements in farming techniques and by enclosure laws—had to work long hours in factories

1798

Napoleon invades Egypt; *Lyrical Ballads* by William Wordsworth and Samuel Taylor Coleridge is published

1799

The Directory is overthrown and Napoleon is named First Consul of the new government

1804

Napoleon crowns himself emperor; Ludwig van Beethoven completes his Third Symphony; the French invent the mechanical loom for weaving designs

1806

Napoleon dissolves the Holy Roman Empire; gas lighting for interior illumination is introduced

1811

Friedrich Ludwig Jahn, the father of gymnastics, opens his first gymnasium

1812

Napoleon invades Russia; the Grimm brothers publish *The Children's and Household Tales*; Byron's *Childe Harold's Pilgrimage* takes London by storm under grueling conditions. Yet even the poorest of Britain's citizens usually were able to find work and could also enjoy some of the benefits of the Industrial Revolution: For example, as goods were produced more cheaply, they were affordable for many more people.

Springing from these revolutions and the dramatic new world they were creating was the intellectual and artistic sensibility called Romanticism. Breaking with rational, Enlightenment ideology, the Romantics were ardent and individualistic, seeking inspiration from heroes and grand events, untamed nature and far-off lands, and a golden past. So inspired, artists of the Romantic era created magnificent and visionary works.

German composer Ludwig van Beethoven infused his music with a sense of heroic grandeur and towering passions. He expressed his fervent belief that "music is . . . the wine which inspires one to new generative processes, and I am the Bacchus who presses out this glorious wine for mankind and makes them spiritually drunken."

Poet William Wordsworth wandered the rolling hills of the English countryside and created lyrical verses about the wonders he found there:

. . . Therefore am I still
A lover of the meadows and the woods,
And mountains; and . . . recognize
In nature and the language of the sense,
The guide, the guardian of my heart, and soul
Of all my mortal being.

More exotic scenery fascinated readers of *Childe Harold's Pilgrimage,* Lord Byron's narrative poem based on his adventures in Greece, Albania, and other regions of the Ottoman Empire. The worlds Byron evoked so powerfully in words were brought to stunning life by artists such as Eugène Delacroix, whose paintings of Greek fighters in Missolonghi—where Byron died—and women in Algiers pulse with vibrant colors. Other artists, such as J. M. W. Turner and

1813	1814	1815	1818	1820	1822
Germaine de Staël's influential *On Germany,* introducing German culture to the rest of Europe, is published in England	Allied forces invade Paris and force Napoleon to abdicate; the Congress of Vienna convenes	Napoleon retakes power but is defeated at Waterloo and permanently exiled; the Bourbons are restored to the French throne	Mary Shelley publishes the horror novel *Frankenstein*	Percy Bysshe Shelley's lyrical drama *Prometheus Unbound* is published	English scientist Michael Faraday invents the electric motor; Percy Bysshe Shelley drowns off the coast of Italy

John Henry Fuseli, sought to stir the viewer's emotions by portraying nature's fury or the terrors of their own dreams and visions. The Grimm brothers looked to the past, setting down the primitive beauty of their heritage in their collected tales peopled with magical beings, evil stepmothers, and hair-climbing kings.

In the 1840s, the volatile political situation that paralleled these passionate artistic endeavors moved toward another explosion. The anger of the French people at corruption in their government and the loss of Revolutionary ideals erupted in 1848, and once again the monarchy became a republic. This event precipitated several insurrections in the German states, where participants issued a call for reforms and the creation of a strong national government. But the changes wrought by these latest uprisings, both French and German, proved to be temporary. A new Napoleon, a nephew of the first, soon proclaimed himself emperor, and the movement for a united Germany fell apart.

Despite the political revolutions of the last 60 years, the old order had once again asserted itself. But its days were numbered. The ideas that came of age between 1789 and 1848 had moved Europe closer to the time when most leaders would find it necessary to give citizens a voice and a constitution.

The Industrial Revolution continued to foment societal change. This revolution steamed into the German states as the second half of the 19th century began, two decades after starting its trek across France. In Britain, though, it had reached journey's end, having accomplished its goal of readying the country for the modern age.

Like the political revolutionaries and the industrialists, the Romantics, whose voices had fallen silent now, would leave the world an enduring legacy. That legacy can be found not only in their magnificent creations but also in the remembrance of a spirit that was, in Samuel Taylor Coleridge's words, "a light, a glory, a fair luminous cloud enveloping the earth . . . that from the soul itself must issue forth."

1824
Beethoven composes his ninth and final symphony; Byron dies in Missolonghi, Greece

1825
Great Britain establishes its first regular passenger rail service

1830
The Bourbon Restoration ends in a coup d'état; the "citizen king," Louis-Philippe, is enthroned as the July monarchy begins; Victor Hugo stages the Romantic drama *Hernani*

1832
The English Reform Bill passes after a near-revolution

1833
French officials make primary education a governmental responsibility

1848
Karl Marx publishes *The Communist Manifesto;* revolutions sweep France and the German Confederation

N

RUSSIA

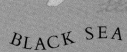

BLACK SEA

HELLESPONT E M P I R E

In the late 18th and early 19th centuries, French armies imposed a new order on Europe. Napoleon crossed the Alps to deprive Austria of its northern Italian territories, dissolved the Holy Roman Empire and created the French-ruled Kingdoms of Holland and Westphalia as well as the Confederation of the Rhine, conquered Spain, and annexed the Papal States in the central part of modern-day Italy. The loss of most of the French army in the Russian campaign of 1812, however, resulted in Napoleon's defeat by European allies and the return of much of Europe to its previous political divisions. One of the lasting effects of Napoleon's attempt to conquer Europe, however, was the formation of the so-called German Confederation.

Europe's changing political landscape was mirrored by changes in the world of art. In Paris, Eugène Delacroix and Antoine-Jean Gros explored new styles of painting; in glittering Vienna, Beethoven and Franz Schubert composed timeless masterpieces; in Coppet, Switzerland, Germaine de Staël wrote books that would earn her the appellation "high priestess of Romanticism"; in German Kassel, the Grimm brothers gathered their folk tales; and in England, William Wordsworth walked the hills near Nether Stowey and explored the lakes and mountain peaks around Grasmere, drawing inspiration from nature. Romantic artists also embarked on grand tours, seeking adventures that would color their work. Lord Byron wandered the streets of Lisbon, traveled through the Albanian mountains by caravan, explored the ruins of Athens, swam the Hellespont, and went home to write his masterpiece, *Childe Harold's Pilgrimage.*

CHAPTER ONE

Passion in Turbulent Times

A winged statue of Fame, perched atop a 72-foot-high column, gazes out over the Place du Châtelet, a bustling square in early-19th-century Paris. The monument honors French soldiers who died in Napoleon's Egyptian campaign during the late 1790s. The French Revolution, Napoleon's springboard to power, also gave birth to Europe's Romantic era.

On a steamy August morning in 1792, along narrow, muddy lanes and trash-littered alleys, Paris housewives were completing their customary shopping in the markets. The banks of the River Seine swarmed with laborers arriving to pursue their daily tasks in tanneries, breweries, dyeworks, the Réveillon wallpaper factory, and Gobelins tapestry workshops. Meanwhile, milliners and haberdashers on the Rue St. Denis cut and stitched cloth sold to them by tradespeople in Montmartre, who in turn were supplied by cotton mills to the west of the city. It was business as usual for much of France's capital, despite the bloody revolution and social upheaval that had begun three years earlier.

The day was anything but usual for 38-year-old Charles-Maurice de Talleyrand, who sat in the office of French minister of justice Georges Danton, listening intently. Danton had called for Talleyrand shortly after being appointed minister on August 13. That was the day when the radicals, tiring of the slow pace of legislative reform, had unleashed an enraged rabble to take direct action. Armed with pikes and lances, the mob had overrun the Tuileries Palace. Upon discovering that King Louis XVI and Queen Marie-Antoinette had fled, they had hacked to pieces the troops guarding the royal abode. The Legislative Assembly, to which the king and queen had turned for protection, promptly deposed the monarchs and established a Provisional Executive Council to rule in their place.

As minister, Danton considered one of his first tasks to be justifying to other countries the events of that momentous day. He had eagerly sought the counsel of Talleyrand, who had returned earlier in the summer from a mission to London, where he had deftly negotiated with Prime Minister William Pitt on behalf of the new French government. Now Danton asked Talleyrand to write a letter to the British government to convince it of the justice of the Revolutionary cause.

To Talleyrand, Danton's request presented an unexpected opportunity—for escape. Bishop, aristocrat, and seasoned diplomat, Talleyrand had been among those who had launched the Revolution in 1789. He had served as president of France's new legislative body, which had pressed forward on government reform. But disturbed by recent events, he had resigned on July 13. Now he had no protection from those hunting suspected counterrevolutionaries, particularly aristocrats and clergy.

If he wanted to live, Talleyrand had to get out of France, so he made Danton an offer. He would compose such a letter if the minister would give him a passport to travel to England as a government envoy. He offered a rationale to justify the trip: Recently he had proposed that a uniform system of weights and measures be adopted internationally. In England, he argued, he could enlist support for his plan from those influential in scientific circles. Danton listened but was not fooled. He knew Talleyrand only wanted to flee. Yet he needed the bishop's help and so agreed to the terms.

After fulfilling his part of the agreement, Talleyrand waited anxiously for Danton to keep his word. The long August days passed with no message from Danton, as prisons continued to be filled with nobles and priests. On September 1, Talleyrand heard the frightening news that a mob had descended upon the prisons and, after holding a series of mock trials, had butchered some

1,200 people. Thus it was with overwhelming relief that five days later he finally received his precious permit bearing the lifesaving words, "Let Talleyrand pass . . . en route to London by our orders."

Only fear for his life could have compelled Talleyrand to emigrate. Son of the count de Talleyrand, Charles belonged to a family as ancient and distinguished as that of the king. He did not grow up in the family home, however, for after his christening, he was sent to stay with a poor woman who lived in an outlying district of Paris. Such fostering was not unusual among French aristocrats, who thus freed themselves from the daily responsibility of child rearing.

While under the peasant's care, the four-year-old Charles fell and dislocated his foot. He received no medical attention and from then on walked with a limp. Despite the injury, the Talleyrands did not bring their son home to Paris, placing him instead in the care of his great-grandmother, the princess de Chalais. The boy grew to love and admire her and, under her care, learned how to read and write, act like a gentleman, and understand the duties of an aristocrat.

For the princess, duty included tending to the medical needs of the tenants on her vast estate in southwestern France. Each Sunday after Mass she held court in a room of her château known as the surgery. The shelves there were crammed with large jars of ointments, elixirs, and syrups, as well as boxes of other medications, prepared once a year by the village surgeon and vicar. A pair of nuns questioned patients and prescribed the necessary medication. Each sick person was introduced to the princess, who sat in a velvet armchair, and if bandages were needed for the patient, Talleyrand brought his great-grandmother a roll of linen from which she herself cut the required strip.

In 1762, Talleyrand's parents brought him to Paris to attend school. Still in no hurry to see him, they sent a family valet to meet his coach and escort him to the lodging of a cousin with whom he would live. Later he would bitterly reflect, "I was then eight years old and the eyes of my parents had not yet rested on me." Indeed they did not visit him during his entire seven years of schooling, although they allowed him to dine with them once a week.

Because of Talleyrand's limp, his parents decided that he was not fit for the army, which was the traditional occupation of those members of his family who did not own great estates. Like many of the nobility, the count and countess had titles but little wealth. Fortunately, their rank entitled them to appointment to high offices at court, with all of the attendant financial and other perquisites. So at age 15 he was pressed to take the path he least desired: entering a seminary. He was told that the Catholic Church was considered a fine starting place for a career in public service and a high position at court and that, despite any vows to the contrary, he did not have to give up luxury or the pleasures of the flesh. Thus assured, after becoming a priest Talleyrand flaunted his pleasure-seeking vices, openly entertaining his mistresses and the more worldly of his peers.

In 1788, Talleyrand was appointed bishop of Autun. The following year, he won election to the Estates-General, a national legislative body composed of three classes of the populace—aristocrats, clergy, and commoners. Talleyrand set off for Paris to claim his seat, still unaware that his country was on the brink of revolution.

Because France was on the verge of bankruptcy, the Estates-General was meeting for the first time in 175 years. Louis XVI and his finance minister had proposed levying a new general tax to relieve the situation, but Parisian and provincial officials had refused to implement it, claiming that taxes could rightfully be imposed only by those who had to pay them. Louis was forced to convene the Estates-General.

The first meeting occurred in May 1789, but the discussions fell apart when the First and Second Estates—the clergy and the aristocrats—tried to arrange matters so that they could always outvote the Third Estate (the commoners) despite the latter's numerical advantage of 595 members to 582. In June 1789, the angry members of the Third Estate declared that they alone formed the National Assembly of French People and set about drawing up a constitution. Many aristocrats, who had been chafing under the absolute power of the king, enthusiastically joined the commoners in their

"He was a strange man," said writer Victor Hugo of Charles-Maurice de Talleyrand *(above)*, "feared and respected . . . and he limped like the devil himself." The comte de Mirabeau sneered, "He would exchange his soul for a pile of dung, and he would be right to do so." Aristocrat, bishop, libertine, revolutionary, and kingmaker, Talleyrand left his mark on regimes in France from the Revolution to the July monarchy.

drive for a constitutional monarchy similar to the British system of government. Talleyrand, ever the pragmatist, supported the move, which he saw as the only hope for the country's stability.

The National Assembly declared an end to the old regime and issued the Declaration of the Rights of Man and of the Citizen, a document which set forth the people's claims to liberty, equality, the inviolability of property, and the right to resist oppression. The practice of feudalism was abolished. At Talleyrand's urging, the assembly seized all church property to help alleviate the financial crisis.

In 1791, the terms of France's first constitution transformed the country into a constitutional monarchy. But then the Jacobins—the radical republicans—began to gain power. In August 1792 they imprisoned the royal family, and the newly elected National Convention then drafted

another new constitution, which abolished the monarchy and declared France to be a republic. Soon after these developments, Talleyrand again fled to England.

France and its government would be repeatedly transformed in the coming decades. At century's end, the republicans were swept from power by Napoleon Bonaparte. In 1814, Napoleon was overthrown and a member of a French royal family, the Bourbons, again ascended the throne, though his rule was tempered

Ignoring their illicit lovers, a husband and wife seeking a divorce are encouraged by a judge to set aside their differences and their passions for their child's sake. Many couples in the 1790s eagerly availed themselves of France's first divorce law, which took effect in 1792.

by a governmental charter. But many people were unhappy under the so-called Restoration as it veered toward a return to absolute monarchy. In 1830, the Bourbon Restoration fell to the July monarchy and its constitutional king. Still, discontent continued to grow, and in 1848 revolution once again swept the country.

In France, the period from 1789 to 1848 also saw many changes in the social order. Women, for instance, fought for new legal and educational rights. In the early 1790s, French-women, inspired by the Revolutionary ideas of equality, formed their own political clubs and pushed for rights such as the right to bear arms. Men in government, outraged and fearful, responded by outlawing the clubs and refusing to grant the requested rights.

Greater personal freedom was increasingly allowed in other areas. Determined to achieve a complete split with the church, the Legislative Assembly declared in 1792 that only civil marriages would be recognized. People who wanted to wed appeared before a bureaucrat who uttered a few encouraging words and pronounced them married. In a still more radical move, the government allowed divorce, after centuries of Catholic tradition that held marriage to be unbreakable.

The turbulence of war and political instability would affect more than government. Doubt was cast upon the rationalist ideas of order, harmony, and reason—ideas which had dominated the preceding period, the Enlightenment. From this would arise the artistic and intellectual movement called Romanticism. The Romantics would promote individual creativity over Classical rules, exalt emotion over reason, love the wild beauty of nature and exotic, far-off places, closely examine the human personality, and admire genius and heroism. The ideas of Romanticism suited many of those who desired

CHAMPIONING THE RIGHTS OF WOMEN

British writer Mary Wollstonecraft *(left)* moved to Paris in December 1792 to see firsthand if the ideals that fueled the Revolution had indeed resulted in major changes in society. Such changes were critical issues for Wollstonecraft, who had dedicated her life to human rights.

Before leaving England, she had published *Vindication of the Rights of Woman,* in which she lamented the helplessness of women and called for their complete civil and political rights. "I do not wish them to have power over men; but over themselves," she declared. Considered radical, the book infuriated many in England; novelist Horace Walpole called Wollstonecraft "a hyena in petticoats."

Wollstonecraft's theories took root in her own unhappy childhood as she watched her domineering father mistreat her mother. She escaped from his tyranny at 19 and set out to support herself, first as a lady's companion and teacher, then as a writer.

While in Paris, Wollstonecraft took an American lover and subsequently bore a child, Fanny, out of wedlock. The affair ended badly, and when France grew too dangerous for foreigners in 1795, Wollstonecraft returned to London. There she married philosopher William Godwin. In 1797, at age 38, she died of fever after giving birth to her second daughter, Mary, who grew up to write the novel *Frankenstein.*

immediate and dramatic change. Thus the two movements—the intellectual stir of Romanticism and the political drive to revolution—would feed upon one another.

Into the maelstrom of competing ideas and passionate acts would vault a host of dashing personalities. Among them were Germaine de Staël, a writer considered the high priestess of French Romanticism, whose outspoken beliefs earned her Napoleon's enmity; Élisabeth Vigée-Lebrun, painter to Marie-Antoinette who would return from exile to support the Restoration; Marc-Antoine Jullien, a former partisan of the Reign of Terror who would dedicate himself to educational and social reform; Alexis de Tocqueville, historian and politician, who would be caught up in the 1848 revolution; and Talleyrand, who would return to Paris to make and break others who sought positions of power.

Talleyrand's exile lasted four years. During that time, France continued to struggle through waves of political upheaval. The leader of the Committee of Public Safety, Maximilien Robespierre, loosed the Reign of Terror, which raged through France from March 1793 to July 1794. Some 43,000 people were executed, among them Louis XVI. Fortunately, Robespierre's fellow National Convention members finally turned against him, and his own execution in July brought an end to the Terror. The bloodshed did not stop completely, for Marie-Antoinette was beheaded in October. In August 1795, a new French constitution established the Directory, which consisted of a five-man council, led by Paul de Barras, that wielded executive power over a larger legislative body.

At the same time, the French were battling other countries fearful of the threat the Revolution represented to their own governments. In 1792, France fought and defeated allied Austria and Prussia, only to find itself combatting a new coalition—composed of Austria, Prussia, Britain, and Spain—the following year.

The English Parliament then passed legislation expelling the French émigrés, including Talleyrand, who sailed to the United States to live. From there he wrote his friend Germaine de Staël, "If I must spend another year here I shall die." As one of the most successful salon hostesses in Paris, she had the ear of many men in power and set to work on his behalf. She succeeded in persuading Barras to let Talleyrand return home to France.

Arriving in Paris in 1796, Talleyrand found a people worn out with revolt and working hard at creating merriment. The social elite was now the middle class. As before the Revolution, those who

In a room decorated with silk draperies and a fine carpet, wealthy Parisians socialize, flirt, and play cards at the turn of the century. When the bloody turmoil of the Revolutionary years ended, people began to acquire luxury items and fill their calendars with engagements at salons, theaters, and dances. Restaurants proliferated as chefs displaced from aristocratic households opened their own establishments.

were flourishing enjoyed innumerable luxuries, while many others barely survived on a daily slab of bread or a few ounces of rice. People were more interested in money than in revolution, and a craze for dancing held everyone in thrall. Talleyrand wrote that "balls and spectacles and fireworks have replaced prisons and revolutionary committees." Those in the forefront of the new lifestyle called themselves the *merveilleuses,* the marvelous ones.

Even Talleyrand was shocked by merveilleuse fashions: Women wore tunics designed to make them look like Greek nymphs, with virtually every part of the body visible through flowing robes of diaphanous muslin. Yet although a woman's body could be casually displayed, her hair had to be hidden. Well-to-do women kept collections of at least 10 wigs, which they changed frequently throughout the day. Men wore frock coats with long skirts over loose-fitting breeches, and elaborate cravats rose from their necks to hide their lower lips. Their ears, sporting golden rings, peeked out from cascading locks of long hair, while other tresses were pinned up in the back with a comb. The male costume was completed by a wide-brimmed hat and a rod of knotted wood nicknamed "executive power," which was likely to be wielded at the slightest insult.

From the time of Talleyrand's return, de Staël campaigned to have him made minister of foreign affairs. In July 1797 Barras arranged it. However, Talleyrand had a clear vision for France's future, and Barras was not the man he saw implementing his vision. Casting about for a powerful young leader who could rise above factional disputes, Talleyrand turned an eye toward General Napoleon Bonaparte, who was then leading a successful campaign against Austria. (Prussia and Spain had made peace with France by this time.) In October, Bonaparte wrested northern Italy from Austrian control, and Talleyrand sent him a flattering letter. A genial correspondence began between the two men, who would meet for the first time when Bonaparte visited Paris that December.

In 1798 Bonaparte took his army—and a research team of scholars and scientists—to Egypt, hoping to ruin British trade in the Mediterranean. Though he won victories over local forces, his fleet was destroyed by the British navy and his army had to continually suppress local uprisings.

Back in Paris, the Directory was falling apart, wracked by factionalism. Talleyrand resigned from the weak, nearly bankrupt government in the summer of 1799 and began plotting a coup d'état. Fortuitously for Talleyrand's plans, Bonaparte returned from his Egyptian military campaign early in October. The expedition had been a failure, but word of the debacle had not reached the French people, who continued to see Bonaparte as a hero.

Talleyrand first persuaded Barras to reform the Directory by setting up a system in which there would be a single director. Then he maneuvered to get Bonaparte the position. Finally, in December, Talleyrand engineered the abolition of the Directory altogether, establishing in its place the so-called Consulate. Bonaparte was named to serve for 10 years as First Consul. The new charter, devised by Talleyrand, called for a total of three consuls but ensured that the other two consuls would be little more than advisers. As his reward, Talleyrand became Bonaparte's foreign minister and chief adviser.

The First Consul took a firm stand against the post-Revolutionary moral laxity, wishing to impose upon France not only order but also propriety. It was a concept to which Talleyrand, who by now had several former mistresses and bastard sons, could not readily subscribe. But in 1802 Bonaparte gave his chief adviser an ultimatum: Give up the current mistress—tall, blue-eyed beauty Catherine Grand—or wed her. Talleyrand chose the latter.

Talleyrand may have agreed to the marriage, but the Catholic Church, with which Bonaparte was currently concluding a reconciliation agreement known as the Concordat, did not. Even though Talleyrand had been defrocked, he had taken a vow of chastity all those years ago, and Pope Pius VII was determined

Archaeologists, brought to Egypt in 1798 by Napoleon Bonaparte, measure the Sphinx *(right)*. Napoleon took along scientists, archaeologists, and artists on his military campaigns so they could explore antiquities, record their findings, and bring back artifacts. Perhaps their greatest find was the Rosetta stone, which was the key to deciphering Egyptian hieroglyphics. On other campaigns, scholars chose from among the world's most prized artworks for the Musée Napoleon (now the Louvre). Above, the emperor and his entourage attend a special illuminated viewing of the confiscated Hellenistic sculpture *Laocoön* at the Musée in 1810.

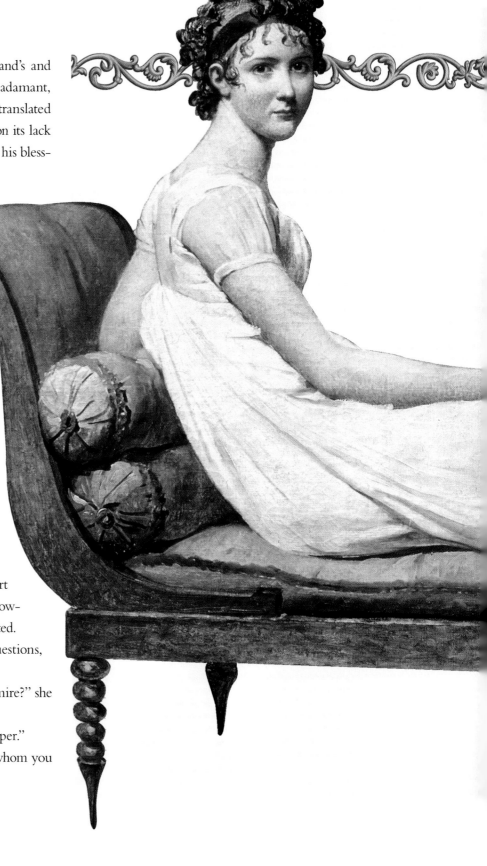

to hold the former bishop to it. Despite all of Talleyrand's and Bonaparte's efforts to bend his will, the pope remained adamant, stating his ruling in a papal brief. This paper, when translated into French, seemed somewhat ambiguous. Seizing upon its lack of clarity, Bonaparte announced that the pope had given his blessing, and Grand and Talleyrand were quickly wed.

The pope was furious, but for the sake of regaining the church's powerful position in France, he made little more of the matter. Indeed, when in 1804 Bonaparte declared himself Emperor Napoleon I, that very same pope would have willingly placed the crown of gold laurel leaves upon the ruler's brow had Napoleon not done so for himself. Talleyrand was made grand chamberlain of the imperial court, and his career continued to flourish during the First Empire.

Unlike Talleyrand, Germaine de Staël did not prosper politically under Napoleon. Indeed, the two became bitter adversaries. That had been far from the writer's intention, however, when she met the French leader at a party at Talleyrand's house on January 3, 1798. Eager to speak with Bonaparte, whom she admired, de Staël asked a mutual friend, Vincent Arnault, to escort her to the general's side. Arnault tried to dissuade her, knowing that Bonaparte disliked learned women, but she insisted.

De Staël proceeded to ply Bonaparte with questions, ignoring his growing hostility.

"Who is [the woman] whom you could most admire?" she asked him.

He responded, "The one who is the best housekeeper."

"Very well," she replied. "But who is the woman whom you would consider most distinguished among her sex?"

Empire Style

To realize his vision of Paris as a city that was "something fabulous, colossal, never-before-seen," Napoleon had triumphal arches, fountains, and temples erected and chose the architects Pierre Fontaine and Charles Percier to refurbish the Tuileries and other palace interiors. The royal residences were filled with luxurious furnishings, fixtures, and textiles crafted by the finest cabinetmakers, metalworkers, silversmiths, and weavers in France. The emperor also commissioned the most gifted painters, sculptors, and artisans of the time to create dazzling works of art glorifying his country and his reign. These artistic endeavors captured the grandeur of the Napoleonic age, together creating a magnificent style that came to be known as Empire.

Empire style was rooted in the prevailing Neoclassicism, which echoed the splendors of ancient Greece and Rome. Representations of Greek and Roman deities and heroic figures appeared on many vases, inkstands, mirrors, and wall reliefs. One mahogany washstand sported decorative motifs copied from treasures found in the Temple of Isis when it was unearthed at Pompeii. An enormous table centerpiece, 12 feet in length, was carved to reproduce the facade of an Egyptian temple, complete with seated pharaohs. There were gilded bronze candelabra molded in the image of the *Winged Victory*, candlesticks shaped like Egyptian water carriers, and even a sugar bowl made of gold and blue enameled porcelain, decorated with illegible hieroglyphics. Potters painted Egyptian scenes on fine porcelain from the national factory in Sèvres.

Weavers from France's textile center at Lyon produced fabulous silks, damasks, brocades, and simulated leopard skin to be used for upholstering chairs, couches, and beds and for tapestries and wall hangings. Furniture was often made of deep, rich

In a celebrated portrait by David, legendary French beauty and salon hostess Juliette Récamier, clad in a flowing Grecian gown of white muslin, reclines on her *méridienne,* or chaise longue. When Empress Joséphine adopted the Classical style, it became the standard for ladies' clothing.

mahogany or gilded and lacquered wood, with the arms and legs of chairs and tables carved into winged lions, the claws of beasts, or, for a lighter touch, swans.

Clothing was also influenced by the Empire style. Empress Joséphine was the arbiter of ladies' fashion, often wearing low-cut, high-waisted dresses with short, puffy sleeves. Light, flowing Roman- and Greek-style tunics had been popular for some time, but Joséphine added a pleated train in the back and borders of fine lace or gold embroidery, which lent a more formal, sumptuous appearance to her cotton percale, muslin, or satin gowns. She also liked to wear a shawl made of cotton or cashmere draped around her shoulders and antique-style ornaments or combs in her hair. Joséphine's manner of dress was emulated by all fashionable Frenchwomen of her day.

At its best, Empire style was elegant, luxurious, and graceful. Unfortunately, it also had a tendency to be gaudy—overdecorated with mythological scenes, allegorical symbols, Egyptian motifs (in vogue at the time), or imperial and patriotic emblems such as bees, stars, or eagles. Other than in clothing, the style remained popular throughout France even after Napoleon's fall and was still used in furnishings and decor until the mid-19th century.

Greek mythological hero Jason grips the Golden Fleece on this bronze clock, designed to be placed on a mantelpiece or console. Clockmaking was one of many industries producing Empire-style *objets d'art.*

On this gilded silver wine cooler with mermaid-shaped handles, a winged cherub plays a flute while sitting contentedly on the back of a lyre-strumming centaur.

Three winged Egyptian sphinxes with clawed feet form the pedestal of a small marble-topped table. Called gueridons, such tables sometimes had tops that could be rotated or tilted to one side for easy storage.

Many a man would have answered with de Staël's own name, but an irritated Bonaparte said, "The one who bears the greatest number of children." Then he bowed, kissed the humiliated de Staël's hand, and took his leave.

Napoleon Bonaparte may have thought little of Germaine de Staël, but others would consider her the most remarkable woman of her generation. Born Anne-Louise-Germaine Necker in 1766, she was the daughter of two middle-class, Swiss-born Parisians: Jacques, a shrewd finance minister, and his wife, Suzanne, a former teacher who conducted one of Paris's leading salons.

Suzanne Curchod had been taught Latin, Greek, geometry, and physics—an unusual education for a girl—by her father, a pastor in a small Swiss village. After his death, she had used that learning to earn a living in the two professions open to a woman of her class: teacher and governess. She had met and married Jacques Necker while working in Paris.

Suzanne Necker wanted her daughter to be exceptional and decided to educate her personally. She isolated the young girl from other children and gave her intensive instruction in mathematics, theology, languages, history, and geography. So difficult was the regimen that Germaine suffered a nervous breakdown at age 13, and Suzanne stopped tutoring her. Though Germaine would go on to become a serious contender in the world of ideas, her mother would always remain critical of the outcome of her efforts. When her daughter's intellectual attainments were praised years later, Suzanne answered, "It is nothing, absolutely nothing beside what I had hoped to make of her."

Germaine's education had also included attendance at her mother's famous salons. Seated on a low wooden stool beside her mother's armchair, Germaine had listened to the conversations of the leading intellectuals of the day. As a result, the matters that had filled her child's mind were hardly those typical of her age.

A middle-aged Germaine de Staël wears an Egyptian-style turban, a fashion introduced in France during the Consulate. Considered by many to be one of the greatest writers of her age, de Staël helped spread the ideas of Romanticism.

At age five, she had inquired of an elderly woman, "What do you think about love?"

Love was something Germaine would pursue throughout her life. In 1786 she married Erik de Staël, a Swedish baron and ambassador to France. She found she could not love him, and after the birth of a daughter a year later, Germaine looked elsewhere for emotional fulfillment. There were several possibilities, for her admirers were legion. Though she was by no means beautiful, her personality was magnetic. She radiated charm, and her conversation was punctuated, said an admirer, by "dashing expressions, witty sallies, and lively and profound thoughts." In 1788, after having a brief affair with Talleyrand, de Staël fell for Louis, vicomte de Narbonne, who would father her first son, Auguste, born in 1790.

These years were exciting for de Staël in other ways as well. She had supported the Revolution and the idea of a constitutional monarchy and delighted in being at the center of the ferment. Her salon at the Swedish Embassy surpassed that of her mother and was the focal point of political intrigue. With the help of influential friends, she succeeded in having Narbonne made war minister in 1791.

But the game changed as the more radical elements, whose actions she did not approve, came to power. When the Jacobins threatened her friends' lives, she secreted several at the Swedish Embassy for protection, among them Narbonne. In late August 1792, a cadre of soldiers arrived at her door demanding the right to search the place. Frantically de Staël concealed Narbonne under the altar in the embassy chapel, then raced to the entrance, where she found a swarm of soldiers about to enter. Ever persuasive, she managed to turn them away, then quickly arranged for Narbonne to have safe passage to England. Not long after, she, too, left France.

In May 1795, with the Terror ended, Madame de Staël returned to Paris with her new lover, Benjamin Constant, who would become a prominent author. Still concerned about the country's future, she tried to persuade the republican and royalist parties to come together for the sake of France. The government, suspicious of her involvement with royalists, exiled her. She was miserable, for she passionately loved Paris. While living at her family estate in Coppet, Switzerland, she wrote, "The universe is in France; outside it, there is nothing."

De Staël was also passionate about words, which, she once noted, could become "an instrument one likes to play and which revives the spirit." She was a prolific writer, jotting down thoughts continually, as a friend observed, "while her hair is being dressed, while she breakfasts, in fact during a third of the day." By the turn of the century, she had written 15 books.

Among them was *A Treatise on the Influence of the Passions upon the Happiness of Individuals and of Nations,* published in 1796, a reflection on the powerful emotions unleashed by national events such as the Reign of Terror. In it, she defends the ideals of the Revolution while deploring the bloody direction taken by the Jacobins; the work establishes a relationship between politics and the heart as well as a connection between history and feelings. The book was destined to become one of the most important works of European Romanticism.

The following year, de Staël was allowed to return to Paris.

She moved into the Swedish Embassy with her husband in order to be with him for the birth of her child—a daughter named Albertine—even though Constant may have been the father. Not even giving birth prevented her from gathering people around her. One visitor reported, "Madame de Staël has at last given birth to her daughter, and at no time did she have fewer than fifteen persons in her room."

In 1800 de Staël published one of her greatest works, *On Literature Considered in Its Relationship to Social Institutions.* Of the book, she wrote, "I propose to examine the influence of religion, morals, and laws upon literature, and the influence of literature upon religion, morals, and laws." It covered a variety of subjects such as the individual versus the state; freedom of thought; and educational, scientific, and moral progress.

According to de Staël, the advancement of civilization requires intellectual growth as well as sensitivity. For the human mind to progress, it must be free of political control. Progress in literature is dependent on the form of government under which writers live. Democracies, she claimed, reduce writers to producing work for popular taste; aristocracies, in which authors write for the elite, demand higher art but discourage originality and enthusiasm. Worst of all for literature are absolute rulers, who stifle thought, innovation, and freedom.

This last pronouncement angered Bonaparte, who as First Consul had already begun to censor the newspapers and theaters. Performances of Voltaire's *The Death of Caesar* were forbidden, for instance, because of Brutus's speeches condemning dictatorship. But despite the French leader's vocal displeasure, *On Literature* was a success, and people flocked to de Staël's salon in the winter of 1800-1801. She was in heaven, doing what she loved most: conversing about politics, life, and art in her beloved Paris. In her mind, no place in the world compared with the French capital.

Many visitors to Paris in 1800 might have disagreed with de Staël's assessment. The French capital had suffered under a decade of destruction and neglect, by-products of the Revolution. The houses of the nobility had been pillaged, then left to deteriorate. Monuments, damaged in the battles, were ready to collapse. With no money for or attention to street repairs, paving stones were askew and ruts were deep.

Street drains became stopped up with debris, and Parisians had to depend on rainstorms to disperse the household wastes.

In July 1802, a local newspaper urged people to clean up the city: "It is hot, very hot, the street surface is burning, the gutters are stagnant and stink of putridness. Water them, therefore! Your own interest calls for it, and the police have ordered it."

Residents were reluctant to do so. They paid for their water by the pail, buying most of it from the vendors pushing wheel-mounted water casks through the streets. The few wells in the

A hustler *(far left)* who has thrown a wooden plank over a muddy street demands a fee for its use from a Parisian family. The streets of Paris, said a visitor in the early 1800s, were "full of refuse and covered with thick glutinous mud."

A man enjoys his tea in the dining room of an early-19th-century bourgeois home. Wood stoves like this one were usually placed in antechambers and lesser rooms, larger rooms being heated by fireplaces.

city's courtyards and the 60 or so drinking fountains frequently ran dry, so much of the water sold by the vendors came directly from the polluted River Seine.

There were other inconveniences to be endured. At night, the avenues were mostly dark, the city's 4,000 oil-burning street lanterns casting only feeble light. For safety, people leaving theaters after nightfall often hired lantern-bearers to guide them home.

Home was often an apartment in a house occupied by poor and rich residents alike. After the Revolution, many houses were rented floor by floor, with space allocated according to class. Usually, tradespeople had their shops on the ground floor. Immediately above them were the wealthy, then the bourgeoisie, the working class, and the poor. Because most large rooms had drafty fireplaces rather than more efficient wood stoves, all classes

suffered equally from a lack of adequate heating. Even Bonaparte, in an attempt to keep warm, often gave audiences while he leaned against a fireplace mantel.

Relations between Bonaparte and de Staël were certainly chilly—and growing frostier by the year. At first Bonaparte merely resented the power she had in the world of the salons, where many who opposed his policies gathered. But then de Staël began gaining an international audience for her opinions. In 1802, she published her first novel, *Delphine,* about a woman of exceptional spirit and intellect who suffers because she cannot force herself to live according to public opinion. The book's feminist tone, its defense of divorce, and its indictment of society's double standards for women and men offended Bonaparte, who saw it as a condemnation of his government. In fact, in the book's preface, de Staël baldly stated that writers "must address the future, not the present, for they are writing for a France which is enlightened but silent." It was an obvious slap at Bonaparte's censorship policies.

As de Staël's works were acclaimed throughout Europe, Bonaparte realized that the writer had become a force to be reckoned with. In October 1803, he ordered her exiled 110 miles outside Paris. Devastated, she sent letters and emissaries begging him to relent, but he remained adamant. Hearing of her fate, de Staël's father wrote to counsel her: "Lift your head high in adversity and permit no man on earth, be he ever so powerful, to hold you under his boot."

De Staël's unhappy exile would last more than a decade. During that time, she traveled to Germany and England and continued to write. Her books often attacked Bona-

As their leader waves his baton *(below)*, youthful conscripts wave to onlookers and bid fond farewells to loved ones *(far left)*. Parading cheerfully by the triumphal arch of the Porte St. Denis, the young men were going to join Napoleon's forces in 1807. A popular song of the day gave a more sobering perspective, saying, "Conscripts leaving gaily is quite against nature."

parte, whom she called "Robespierre on horseback," and helped maintain Europe's opposition to him. He would become livid at the mention of her name, claiming, "No one is more evil than she."

Napoleon Bonaparte's attitude toward Germaine de Staël was, at heart, the same as his attitude toward all women: They needed to be kept in their place. In March 1804, he passed what would be the cornerstone of his civil administration: the Napoleonic Code. Women were stripped of rights they had gained during the 1790s. A wife could no longer sue for divorce unless her husband brought his mistress home. Men, on the other hand, could demand a divorce for any act of adultery, and if a woman was found guilty of it, she could be imprisoned. Married women were also barred from independently entering into contracts and from bringing suit.

In 1810 de Staël returned to France—though not to Paris—to supervise the publication of her latest book, *On Germany*. Although her work assessed the Germans in a favorable light, it was liberally sprinkled with barbs against Napoleon. Before it could be published, however, *On Germany* had to be submitted for review to the book censorship office the emperor had recently established. Unsurprisingly, Napoleon had the book banned. Then he tried to ensure that it would never be published anywhere. At the emperor's orders, police descended on the plant where de Staël's book was being printed and destroyed the type used to print her manuscript. They also confiscated the galley sheets, which they crushed into pulp.

But de Staël outmaneuvered her powerful adversary by managing to spirit away a set of proofs and several copies of her work. In 1813, *On Germany* was printed in London and became an instant success. This triumph over Napoleon would soon be surpassed by an even greater one, however. In 1814, events would transpire that would allow de Staël to return at last to her beloved city of Paris.

Those events had their roots in 1804. Following his coronation, the emperor had set out to conquer all of western Europe. Hundreds of thousands of men were conscripted into his Grande Armée, which fought one battle after another to expand Napoleon's empire and power. But beginning in 1808, the army began to suffer significant defeats; the French people grew tired of the continuous warfare and death. Then in 1812, Napoleon made a fatal mistake: He attempted to invade Russia. The punishing Russian winter and rampant disease destroyed his army. The returning emperor lost not only his troops but also his popularity, even in Paris. A coalition of European countries, eager to strike at the weakened French leader, advanced on France.

Napoleon was overthrown in the spring of 1814 and was sent to live on the island of Elba off the coast of Italy; he returned in March 1815 and ruled for a brief period called the Hundred Days before being defeated once and for all and sent into permanent exile. Napoleon's banishment would release Germaine de Staël from her own exile. She came home to Paris, where she died in 1817 following a cerebral hemorrhage. One of her most important works, *Considerations on the Principal Events of the French Revolution,* was published posthumously. The book supported the idea of a constitutional monarchy and would become a bible of sorts for French liberals, who hoped that the next government would realize what the Revolution and Napoleon had not.

In March 1814, shortly before Napoleon's first fall from power, Élisabeth Vigée-Lebrun was in her country home in Louveciennes, preparing for bed. The 58-year-old artist loved spending summers in the small town 15 miles outside Paris. "I was won over by the view," she once explained, "so extensive that the eye can follow the course of the Seine for a great distance; by the magnificent woods at Marly, by the delicious orchards, so well tended that one believes oneself in the Promised Land."

Vigée-Lebrun had just slipped into bed when her Swiss servant Joseph burst into her room. Prussians had invaded the village and were now pillaging nearby houses, he warned her. But before she could react, three of the invaders stormed into her room. "Their faces ferociously contorted, they approached my bed brandishing their swords," she later recalled. Joseph "was making himself hoarse shouting in German that I was a Swiss citizen and a sick woman; but they said nothing, and merely helped themselves to a gold snuffbox that lay on my bedside table." For the next four hours, the soldiers roamed around the country home, stripping it of possessions but leaving the artist and her servant unharmed.

Once the Prussians had gone, Vigée-Lebrun attempted to seek refuge in the town of Saint-Germain but soon discovered the roads were unsafe. She found herself sleeping with five other women in a building at nearby Marly that housed a water pump. She could consider herself one of the fortunate. "The country people camped in the vineyards," Vigée-Lebrun later wrote, "and slept on straw in the open air for they had been stripped of everything they owned."

The soldiers at Louveciennes were part of the invasion force sent by Prussia, Austria, Russia, and England to crush Napoleon. On March 30, several days after Vigée-Lebrun's house was ransacked, 70,000 foreign troops attacked Paris. Napoleon was not in the city to meet the invasion; at 2 a.m., the French government officially capitulated. Napoleon's recently appointed vice grand-elector, Charles-Maurice de Talleyrand, who had actually been working secretly to oust the emperor, met with the leaders of the invasion. The French senate subsequently deposed Napoleon and formed a new, provisional government for France, with Talleyrand as its president.

Talleyrand had concluded that enthronement of a Bourbon king was the only hope for France's stability. To achieve this, he had conspired to replace the emperor with the count de Provence, brother of King Louis XVI, a short, fat man who had been living in England, where he called himself Louis XVIII. Louis was offered the throne with the understanding that he would reign under a constitution.

The constitutional charter would provide for a two-house parliament: the Chamber of Peers, drawn by the king from the noble ranks, and the Chamber of Deputies, elected by electoral colleges throughout the country. Electors, of which there would be only about 100,000, would qualify for their position by paying a substantial tax. Those who wished to be eligible to sit in the Chamber of Deputies would have to pay a tax more than three times as high as the tax the electors paid. Louis agreed to the charter but claimed that it was valid only by royal decree and not as a legal document above the Crown. Talleyrand would become the king's foreign minister.

When she heard that Louis soon would arrive in Paris to claim the throne, Vigée-Lebrun, an ardent royalist, set out for the capital. On the Sunday after her arrival, Vigée-Lebrun joined a crowd of well-wishers hoping to catch a glimpse of their new king as he made his way to church. When Louis spotted the artist, whom he had known in pre-Revolutionary days, he stopped to greet her. "He paid me a thousand compliments," she later recorded, adding smugly, "He did not approach any of the other women." It was a glorious moment for one who had begun life as a member of the petite bourgeoisie, or lower middle class.

Born in Paris on April 16, 1755, Élisabeth Vigée was the daughter of portraitist Louis Vigée and his wife, Jeanne, a former hairdresser. The family lived comfortably, though Louis would never command the high prices for his paintings that his daughter would for hers. Nor would he achieve her level of fame, despite his position as first portraitist to Louis XV's mistress Madame de Pompadour.

With her palette and paintbrushes in hand, Élisabeth Vigée-Lebrun works at her easel in this self-portrait, painted in 1790 for the Roman Accademia di San Luca, of which she was a member.

MADNESS: FASCINATION AND REFORM

Believing that there was a connection between madness and genius that ignited the creative spark, Romantic writers and artists often used insanity as a theme. French painter Théodore Géricault created several starkly realistic yet sympathetic portraits of the insane *(above).*

At the same time, society at large was examining madness in a new light, due to the reforms of French physician Philippe Pinel. As head of an insane asylum for men in 1792, Pinel removed the chains that had bound some inmates for 30 to 40 years. In 1794, he did the same in a women's asylum. Instead of treating them as if they were wild beasts, Pinel talked to inmates and provided them with meaningful activities.

At age six, Élisabeth Vigée was sent to board at a convent, where her education undoubtedly was restricted to instruction in morality and social graces (all that girls needed to know, in most people's opinions). But Élisabeth cared more for art than grace. "I doodled constantly and everywhere; . . . on the dormitory walls I sketched figures and landscapes in charcoal, which, as you may imagine, meant I was often in disgrace."

Louis Vigée encouraged his daughter, letting her "dabble with his paints and crayons the whole day long." After Élisabeth left the convent at age 11, her father's artist friends offered her instruction in painting, and Louis invited her to spend time in his studio. Her mother even posed for a seminude portrait by her daughter because female artists were barred from the life-drawing classes at the Académie Royale schools. Life drawing was essential to the pursuit of historical painting, which was then considered the highest genre in pictorial art. Female painters were therefore usually relegated to what were considered the lesser forms: portraiture and still life.

Though her father died when she was 12, Élisabeth's artistic career continued, and while still a teenager, she began to get commissions for paintings. In 1776, she wed the painter and art dealer Jean-Baptiste-Pierre Lebrun, despite her ambivalence about marriage in general. Most women married to obtain financial security, Élisabeth noted, but she wrote, "I had few worries about my future since I was already earning a substantial amount of money." She did worry about losing control of her earnings since under French law they would become her husband's property. In fact, she later claimed that Lebrun's "frenzied passion for women of easy virtue, combined with his passion for gambling, caused the ruin of his fortune and my own." But a strong desire to escape the family home and a stepfather she despised may have been the deciding factor in her choice to accept Lebrun's proposal of marriage.

In 1778, Vigée-Lebrun received her first commission to paint the French queen Marie-Antoinette from life. A warm friendship developed between the two women. It was with Marie-Antoinette's help that Vigée-Lebrun finally received admittance to the Académie Royale. Such membership was a requirement for any artist who wanted to exhibit work at the Salon—Paris's annual art exhibition. Before the queen's intervention, the Académie had refused to offer Vigée-Lebrun full membership, despite the quality of her work and her growing fame. The reasons were twofold: First, her husband was an art dealer, and the Académie thought any association with business compromised painting's status as a liberal art. Second, Vigée-Lebrun was a woman, and the Académie was reluctant to admit female artists. Since 1770, it had restricted the number of women admitted to four at any one time. Fortunately for Vigée-Lebrun, by 1783 there were only two. After the queen suggested that the Académie overlook Lebrun's profession, Vigée-Lebrun received her membership.

In 1789, Vigée-Lebrun's career was flourishing. But France on the verge of revolution was not the place for an ardent royalist and fierce supporter of Marie-Antoinette. Shocked and frightened by the antiroyalist talk, she decided to leave France. Neighbors

After the formation of the Consulate in 1799, Vigée-Lebrun began to consider returning to France. Receiving reassurance from a Consulate official that she could safely do so, Vigée-Lebrun returned to Paris in 1802. But disliking the changes she found in Napoleonic France, missing the charms of the *ancien régime,* she left again almost immediately. For the next several years, she traveled abroad, periodically returning to the French capital. In 1809 she purchased her house in Louveciennes and thereafter divided her time between it and her Paris apartment.

Not all of Vigée-Lebrun's fellow artists felt as she did about Napoleonic France and its leader. Jacques-Louis David, born in Paris in 1748, said of Napoleon Bonaparte: "There is a man to whom altars would have been raised in ancient times." David had ardently supported the Revolution. Appointed to the Commit-

"*There is a man to whom altars would have been raised in ancient times.*"

advised her to travel incognito on the public stagecoach rather than in her private carriage. Around midnight on October 6, her husband and brother escorted her and her nine-year-old daughter, Julie, to the coach, which would take them out of Paris to Lyon, the first leg of their journey to Rome.

Over the next decade, the painter and her daughter lived a life of exile, traveling from country to country. Vigée-Lebrun painted the portraits of many of Europe's nobility and was invited to join several academies. In 1792, the Revolutionary government stripped Vigée-Lebrun and other émigrés of their citizenship. Two years later, during the Terror, her husband divorced her, seeking to protect his person and his property by disassociating himself from his royalist wife.

tee of General Security in 1793, he had signed almost 300 death warrants. He also had been instrumental in abolishing the Académie Royale, which was replaced with the Institut de France, an organization that barred all women from its ranks. Briefly imprisoned after the Reign of Terror, David eventually became Napoleon's official painter and produced several heroic portraits of him. Vigée-Lebrun's relationship with David, unsurprisingly, was antagonistic. He had insultingly called her a lackey of the royal court before the Revolution.

David's art, heroic and realistic, provided a transition between the 18th-century style of Vigée-Lebrun and the passionate art of the Romantic painters, whose ranks included David's student Antoine-Jean Gros. Gros, born in 1771, was attracted to the vivid color—thought to be a dangerously emotive element by Classical artists—and liveliness of Romantic painting and became a leader in its development. It was Gros who took control of David's studio when the latter was exiled after Napoleon's final defeat in 1815.

Vigée-Lebrun, who had known Gros since his childhood, was happy when he was named official portraitist to Louis XVIII. Gros, she wrote, "did not express himself like other men; he always found images that were full of originality and force to convey his thought, and one can say of him that he painted as he spoke." But after 1815, Gros's work suffered when he adopted a more Neoclassical style of painting at the urging of his former teacher David. The change undoubtedly pleased Louis, who preferred the Classical to the Romantic style.

Despite the king's preferences, Romantic art flourished during the 1820s. Ironically, Romantic artists had initially supported Louis because monarchy and Catholicism, which the king championed, evoked the nostalgic past that inspired them. But Louis XVIII, like Napoleon and Louis XVI, wanted art to glorify the government. To create such works, the Romantics averred, would stifle their imaginations.

In the past, artists like Vigée-Lebrun had painted primarily for royal and aristocratic patrons and had focused on Classical and heroic subjects that supported the monarchy. The Romantic artists preferred to paint for themselves, expressing personal truths. They also painted scenes of everyday life to sell to the bourgeoisie, who favored those depictions over renderings of Classical heroes. As one critic wrote, referring to some of David's paintings: "The huge pictures composed of thirty nude figures inspired by antique statues . . . were very respectable works; but . . . they have begun to be a little boring."

Whatever disagreements the king had with other artists, Vigée-Lebrun adored him. In her opinion, Louis had brought civilization back to France. "Though circumstances were difficult, France and its King emerged with dignity from the abyss into which Bonaparte had thrown them," she wrote. She noted, among other things, that Louis enjoyed discussing literature and had written verse in his youth; spoke in Latin with scholars; and loved the Comédie Française, Paris's most important theater.

"I prefer Louis XVIII's civility to Bonaparte's money," said François-Joseph Talma, one of France's leading actors, after meeting the king at the Comédie Française. Though Napoleon had supported the theater during his reign, invited Talma to dine with him several times, and showered the actor with financial rewards, he also restricted the number of theatrical establishments in Paris and heavily censored productions. Under Louis, censorship decreased—a state of affairs actors and writers happily exploited.

During the Restoration, governmental weaknesses and the follies of prominent figures were often lampooned. Fights sometimes broke out between theatergoers of opposing parties: ultras (ultraroyalists), who sought total restoration of the monarchy; liberals, who supported a constitutional monarchy; republicans, who desired a return to Revolutionary principles; and Bonapartists, who were desperate for the enthronement of Napoleon or, after Napoleon's death in 1821, his son. These brawls led to the establishment of the checkroom in France's theaters, where such potential weapons as canes and umbrellas had to be left.

Most of the public preferred the entertainment found in the playhouses on the boulevards to the great productions in state theaters such as the Comédie Française. Here could be found a cornucopia of comedies, farces, and melodramas. One-act sketches were written for all types of occasions, such as commemorating the murder of an important political figure or the addition of a giraffe to Paris's Jardin des Plantes. The most popular playwright in France was Augustin-Eugène Scribe, a master of the French comedy of manners. Scribe was one of the first playwrights to

At the entrance of one of Paris's most popular playhouses, the Théâtre de l'Ambigu-Comique, a guard tries in vain to control a crowd shoving and trampling one another to attend a free performance of the melodrama *La Prise de Jerusalem* in 1819. Since the early 1790s, the government had subsidized theater owners who were willing to offer occasional free performances.

A stagecoach stops to allow a passenger to disembark at a relay
station's inn in the French countryside. Relay posts were positioned
about every 10 miles (as far as a diligence, or coach, could travel in
an hour) so horse teams could be fed and watered or changed. The
stations, especially the ones offering food and drink and overnight
accommodations, were a welcome respite for weary travelers.

portray bourgeois morality and life, and he infused 19th-century French drama with religious and liberal political ideas.

Scribe's work differed greatly from the passionate and melodramatic Romantic plays, which were only beginning to gain popularity near the end of the Restoration period. The first successful Romantic play presented on the stage, in 1829, was *Henri III et sa cour,* about the French Renaissance, written by Alexandre Dumas *père.* The play's massacres, imprisonments, escapes, and murders, inspired by the Revolution, were a startling contrast to more sedate Neoclassical works. Another successful Romantic drama, presented in 1830, was Victor Hugo's *Hernani,* about the 16th-century Netherlands. It mixed history and melodrama with superior lyricism and became a model for Romantics to emulate. Both playwrights would go on to write several more plays as well as popular novels, among them Dumas's *Les Trois Mousquetaires* (The Three Musketeers) and Hugo's *Les Misérables.*

Despite the numerous entertainments found in the city and offered by her friends, Vigée-Lebrun continued to enjoy time in the countryside. After the death of her daughter from illness in 1819 and of her brother the following year, the artist set out on a trip to the port city of Bordeaux, in southern France.

She found the roadways to be well maintained, a vast improvement from the gutted and unrepaired lanes of the Empire days. "I must not forget to mention that the road from Paris to Bordeaux looks exactly like a garden path; it is a permanent road and built so it does not fatigue the traveler in the least." The burgeoning commerce of the period demanded better roads for the increasing number of wagons and carts carrying goods and for the often-overcrowded passenger stagecoaches known as diligences.

Vigée-Lebrun was enchanted with the picturesque seaport of Bordeaux. From her hotel on the water, she wrote, "The view of the other bank stretches as far as a green hillside dotted with a few houses . . . and in the far distance looms a mountain bedecked with castles. . . . There were so many harbored sailing vessels, a thousand smaller ships and boats coming and going in every direction. . . . I never grew tired of [the view], especially in the moonlight; then I could see the flickering lights of the houses on the hillside and the effect was quite magical."

Beneath the magical beauty of Restoration France, trouble was brewing. In 1824, Louis XVIII died and was succeeded by his brother Charles X. Charles wanted a return to the old monarchy, when no constitution impinged upon the king's authority. He would, he stated, "prefer to saw wood than to reign in the manner of the King of England." Despite opposition from the left and the rising discontent among the public, Charles pushed through a press law that severely limited what could be published and campaigned for a stronger Catholic Church. The king increased the power of the ultras, polarizing the political situation. In March 1830, Charles dissolved the Chamber of Deputies, whose majority had just voted to denounce his ministry, and ordered new elections for the summer. Talleyrand, on hearing the news, commented, "Nothing can now prevent a disaster."

Talleyrand and many others knew that the election would change nothing. Talleyrand, of course, had no reason to love the Bourbons. In September 1815, Louis XVIII had allowed him to be forced out of his positions as president of the Council and as foreign minister. Now Talleyrand allied himself with the liberals who wanted to dethrone Charles X and put in his place Louis-Philippe, the duke of Orléans, from a junior branch of the royal family.

That summer of 1830, Talleyrand saw his prediction of disaster come true. In the new election, the opposition won an overwhelming majority of seats in the Chamber. Charles X and his ministry promptly dissolved the Chamber once again, further restricted suffrage, and silenced the press completely. Then, blithely ignoring the political turmoil that ensued, the king left for the country to hunt. In his absence, the opposition struck back.

On July 27, republicans, mostly workers and students, seized control of Paris's streets by erecting more than 5,000 barricades

EMBARKING ON A STORMY SEA

"One's spirit expands with the momentous happenings," wrote Aurore Dudevant on July 31, 1830, referring to both the Paris coup d'état and her introduction to Jules Sandeau, a law student with literary aspirations. The 26-year-old Dudevant subsequently proclaimed herself to be a republican and followed Sandeau to Paris, leaving behind an unhappy marriage. From Paris she wrote, "I am embarking on the stormy sea of literature." Her first solo voyage was the 1832 novel *Indiana*, about a woman who protests the social conventions binding her to an abusive husband, whom she abandons to find love. She published it under a pseudonym, *G. Sand*.

The book was a success, and George Sand, as she became known, went on to earn greater fame with some 60 novels and numerous plays and essays. Yet many people disapproved of her personal life. At times in the 1830s, she wore a waistcoat, boots, and trousers. Her reason: Women's clothes were expensive and impractical for one who walked Paris's muddy streets. She was also notorious for her stormy, very public affairs, most notably with composer Frédéric Chopin and poet Alfred de Musset.

Though Sand's contemporaries might have condemned her private life, they praised her as one of the great Romantic writers. Elizabeth Barrett Browning proclaimed Sand "the finest female genius of any country or age." Mused Honoré de Balzac, "What will become of the world when all women are like George Sand?"

of paving stones with upended carts across them. People defended the barricades against government soldiers with bullets and a rain of furniture, thrown from the upper-story windows of surrounding houses. The battle raged on the next day. As night fell, the government, in desperation, rang the tocsin—the bells of alarm—from Notre Dame and beat drums calling the citizens to arms. Talleyrand, in his Paris lodgings, heard them and turned to a guest.

"Listen! The tocsin! We are winning!"

"We?" inquired the visitor. "Who are 'we'?"

Talleyrand, who had never yet backed the losing side, replied, "I will tell you tomorrow."

The matter became clear on July 29: Charles X's forces had lost. The republicans formed a municipal commission to govern, hoping to persuade the marquis de Lafayette, the venerated French officer and hero of the American Revolution, to lead the country. The liberals, meanwhile, set up their own headquarters and put forward their own candidate, Louis-Philippe, the duke of Orléans. Lafayette, who had previously advocated a constitutional monarchy, supported the duke. On August 2, Charles abdicated.

Talleyrand, once again at the center of things, met with Louis-Philippe late that night to discuss, among other matters, revisions to the constitutional charter. Louis-Philippe had to agree that the charter would no longer be granted by the king but would be a separate legal document. On August 7, the revised charter was accepted by the Chamber. On August 9, Louis-Philippe became the "citizen king." Talleyrand would become his ambassador to England, a post he would hold until he retired in 1834, just four years before his death.

Vigée-Lebrun was devastated by the coup d'état. "This was the family that led us towards the Restoration," she wrote in her memoirs. "I shall leave politicians to explain why virtue and goodness are not sufficient to preserve the throne; my grateful heart can only regret this fact." By the time the artist wrote these memoirs, in the 1830s, her painting career had all but ended. But Vigée-Lebrun herself continued to fascinate people until her death in 1842. A fellow artist commented that if "her painting, at the end of her life, had lost much of its former appeal, her person had remained quite charming, gracious, and even frisky, as she must have appeared to the friends of her youth."

At first, Marc-Antoine Jullien, a 55-year-old liberal, had been thrilled with Charles X's abdication on August 2, 1830. France had a chance to restructure its government and become a true constitutional monarchy. But within days, Jullien's hopes for the future seemed in jeopardy. The Chamber was on the verge of proclaiming Charles's cousin Louis-Philippe "king of the French,"

common sense and foresight, truthful and energetic addressed such language to heads of government during the Revolution, to Napoleon when he was intoxicated by his own pride, genius and success, and to Louis XVIII and Charles X. . . . He was said to be factious, a complainer and malcontent; he was dismissed, persecuted, proscribed, and treated as a veritable pariah. . . . May his voice not be again ignored!"

The Cassandra, or unheeded prophet, of whom Jullien ringingly spoke was himself. And he had indeed been involved with various governments of France since the days of the Revolution—for better or worse. Born into a relatively prosperous bourgeois family in 1775, he had grown up in a small town in the southern province of Dauphiné. At age 10, when Jullien was ready

"One was never sure, between ordering and eating one's dinner, whether a revolution might not intervene."

without first laying the groundwork to protect France from another absolute monarchist. Apparently unaware that Talleyrand was working to alter the charter, Jullien sat at his desk and began writing furiously. On August 6, his warning pamphlet entitled *The Common Sense of the Nation* appeared.

"If you set up a throne before the fundamental law is established you will renew the same great error that threw France, in 1814, into the trap of a royal charter that was improvised and proclaimed only by royal authority," Jullien wrote. "If we hasten too quickly to name a king before arranging for the throne to take root in the law and the nation, the throne will be less solid and more easily shaken." Jullien continued, "A man of

to go off to secondary school in Paris, his loving parents insisted on moving with him.

Since Jullien's father had no need to earn a living, he spent most of his time pursuing his literary and political interests. This led to his joining the Paris Jacobin Club, one of a number of such societies sprouting up throughout France. In January 1792, 16-year-old Jullien, stirred by the political currents, delivered an antiwar speech at his father's club. Blaming the looming war on the king and the royalists, Jullien urged "a final effort to save us from this dreadful scourge."

Jullien's antiwar speech came to the attention of Maximilien Robespierre. In September 1793 he made Jullien a roving agent for the Committee of Public Safety. Violent uprisings had broken out in the cities of Lyon and Marseille, where moderates had seized power from the Jacobins. There had also been conflicts between the two groups in Toulon and Bordeaux, and in late August, royalists had assumed control of Toulon. The committee sent Jullien to work with local leaders to break up conspiracies, bring together warring factions of the Revolutionary forces, and fire up the patriots.

Although earlier he had condemned extremists, Jullien now saw moderate leaders as a problem. They allowed the rich merchants and local gentry to continue their luxurious lifestyle, while the poor lacked employment and often went hungry. In June 1794 he wrote to Robespierre that "the time of crisis has come for Bordeaux" and recommended that the Terror fall "on aristocrats, moderates, intriguers, and federalists." After receiving the

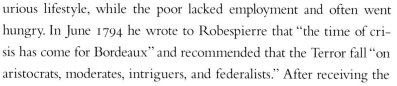

Under the watchful eye of their schoolmaster, young boys walk to school. Primary education in early-19th-century France was woefully inadequate: Textbooks were few, teachers were underpaid and poorly trained, and more time was spent on studying the catechism than on reading or writing. Education laws passed by the July monarchy in the early 1830s sought to correct these problems.

necessary authority, young Jullien oversaw the death by guillotine of some 200 individuals, asserting afterward that the city was at last "purified and regenerated."

When Jullien returned to Paris in August, the tide had turned against Robespierre, who already had been executed, and his agents. Jullien was imprisoned, and only his youth saved him from a death sentence. He did not languish in jail long, however; he was set free with other political prisoners the following year.

Jullien subsequently sought to serve the new national hero, Napoleon Bonaparte, in his successful campaign to conquer northern Italy. In 1797, Jullien was assigned to transport a half-million francs from Venice to Bonaparte's headquarters about 100 miles to the northeast. While crossing from Venice to Trieste, his ship was captured by Austrian privateers. Jullien made an impassioned speech declaring that French vessels cruised nearby to guard his own ship and that he was on an important mission to promote peace. He managed to convince his captors and save his treasure as well as his skin. Commended for his act of bravery, he was appointed by Bonaparte to edit an army newspaper. Yet when Bonaparte later declared himself France's emperor, Jullien was appalled. Napoleon, Jullien wrote in anger, was "an absolute master who absorbs everything into himself." He scribbled these words, however, not in one of the political pamphlets he sometimes published but in one of his numerous private memos. He dared not challenge the emperor publicly, having a wife and children to support. Jullien reined in his own thoughts and, like Talleyrand, continued to work for the French state from the Revolution through the Empire period.

Jullien's employment with the government ended when the Restoration began, but he had other interests to pursue. Since his Revolutionary days, he had been concerned with educational needs and reforms. In 1807 he had published *General Essay on Education,* offering a year-by-year curriculum program for young people. His interest in education dated back even earlier, however. In an 1801 publication called *Appeal to True Friends of the Country,* promoting support for First Consul Bonaparte, Jullien condemned pre-Revolutionary schools for promoting too much frivolity, saying, "Substance was sacrificed to form, ideas to style."

The Jacobins would undoubtedly have agreed with him. In the 1790s, they had promoted the radical idea of free, compulsory education for children in order to produce good republicans. Boys and girls, ages five to 10, would be taught republican virtues and patriotism in primary schools along with reading, writing, and swimming. In the secondary schools, boys between the ages of 10 and 16 would have military and agricultural-science instruction. Older male students would participate in military exercises and help farmers bring in the harvest. But the Jacobins had neither the time nor the money to effectively implement their policies. When the Directory came into power, it eliminated state-funded primary schools and established fee-charging institutions, thus restricting the number of children who could afford to attend.

Primary education did not truly become common throughout the country until after another law was passed in 1833, during the reign of Louis-Philippe. Envisioning a skilled and "civilized" labor force, obedient to the government, the lawmakers at last made primary education a governmental responsibility.

Communities were required to establish primary schools for boys (not until 1850 would primary school for girls be compulsory) and to pay teachers a certain minimum salary. Students would be taught reading, writing, arithmetic, and a standardized form of French, and be given moral and religious training as well. At first, however, only a small percentage of workers' children attended school. Families often could not afford to give up a child's wages. But, gradually, attendance grew.

Literacy, which had been only about 40 percent among adults at the end of the Restoration, began to rise, encouraging an increase in the number of newspapers published in France. Jullien added to the number of news publications with a monthly journal entitled *Revue Encyclopédique,* launched in 1819, for which he was chief editor and contributing writer. He said of the *Revue,* "Its object is to set forth, accurately and faithfully, the march and continuing progress of human knowledge in relation to the social order and its improvement which constitute true civilization."

Jullien was fascinated by technological and scientific advances. One *Revue* article reported on the first steamship to cross the ocean—an 18-day journey from the American port of Savannah, Georgia, to Liverpool, England. The *Revue* also carried articles on, among other subjects, the relatively new art of lithography, suspension bridges, the railroad, and canal building.

In 1833, the *Revue* was forced to cease publication. It was one more unhappy moment in a bad decade for Jullien. He had lost his wife in 1832 after a long illness. Three times during the decade, he ran for a seat in the Chamber of Deputies and lost, indicating that his activities during the Terror were neither forgotten nor forgiven. He also experienced financial troubles and was disillusioned by the July monarchy, with its constitutional king. The new regime, he wrote, "has mistreated so many uncorrupted and disinterested men and made the fortune of so many ambitious intriguers."

Jullien was also disturbed by the July monarchy's ruthless repression of dissidence, including the protests of urban laborers

CAPTURING THE WORLD

When Louis Daguerre *(above)* presented his new method of creating images—named daguerreotype—at a joint meeting of Paris's Académies des Sciences and Beaux-Arts in 1839, an overflowing crowd gathered in the courtyard. Building on an earlier process, Daguerre found a way to create a permanent photographic image on a silver sheet, using far less light-exposure time (20 to 30 minutes, compared with eight hours), and preserve it on a copper plate using a salt solution. He had produced his first successful picture, a still life *(right),* two years earlier.

The public went wild, buying out supplies at local opticians' shops, eager to create their own clear, minutely detailed landscape or architectural rendering. It would be several more years before exposure time was shortened enough for the daguerreotype to be used for portraiture.

who feared loss of employment due to industrialization. In an 1840 tract, *The Voice of France,* he told the government that it need not fear dissent from working classes if it would take necessary action. "If the suffering laboring classes see that attention is paid to their problems, they will cease to feel the anxiety, irritation and hostile attitudes which too often lead to dangerous explosions." The government paid little heed to such advice.

During the early 1840s, other writers and journalists produced a torrent of radical new ideas, mostly in opposition to the effects of the capitalism that supported the ruling class. These ideas were the extreme expression of a general feeling that the ideals of the Revolution had been lost, that France was sinking

into dreary reaction. In the interests of reform, the Revolution was repeatedly revisited by historians, who emphasized its glories and ideals and glossed over its horrors.

Among those historians was Alphonse de Lamartine, an aristocrat and heir to vast estates in Burgundy and a much-acclaimed Romantic poet. As a member of the Chamber, he managed to charm both conservatives and liberals. Lamartine claimed that his eight-volume book on the Revolution, *The History of the Girondins,* was a "protest against the alleged necessity for violence." In fact, the book justified Revolutionary violence and defended Revolutionary heroes, including Robespierre, although it condemned the massacres. The book appeared to great acclaim in 1847 and added to the atmosphere of Revolutionary fervor that was then building in Paris, fueled by disastrous crop failures over two years that sent food prices soaring, inspired hoarding and speculation, and caused widespread unemployment.

During 1847 the opposition parties began holding a series of banquets to demand governmental reform and extension of voting rights. The gatherings were staged as banquets to get around governmental restrictions on political meetings. The most radical elements soon took control of the parties' agenda. At least one such member spent three months ranging across the country, giving speeches on reform and stirring up the populace. Yet Alexis de Tocqueville, like Lamartine a historian and opposition member, warned those who tried, unsuccessfully, to get him involved in the banquets: "If, however, you do start a popular agitation, you have no more idea than I have where it will take you."

Tocqueville certainly had no love for Louis-Philippe. The king, Tocqueville commented, "had a profound understanding of men, but only in respect to their vices. . . . He was by nature fond of power and of dishonest courtiers." But however he felt about the king, he thought the opposition was headed for disaster.

The climactic celebration of the reform banquets was to be held on February 22, 1848, in Paris's 12th arrondissement,

known for its high concentration of radicals. When police prohibited the banquet, violence broke out. Tocqueville, who had been invited to dinner that night, was disturbed to find that only five of 20 expected guests had made it to the gathering. Even the host's wife did not join them, having taken to her bed after a skirmish broke out on the street beneath her window. "I felt we were living in strange times," Tocqueville later wrote, "when one was never sure, between ordering and eating one's dinner, whether a revolution might not intervene."

Rioting worsened when panicky soldiers fired on a mob outside the Ministry of Foreign Affairs, killing 40 people. On February 24, the king abdicated in favor of his grandson, dressed himself in a frock coat and bowler hat, and fled to England.

Tocqueville, Lamartine, and the rest of the deputies rejected Louis's grandson and formed a provisional government. The group was deeply divided between radicals who wanted revolution and socialism and moderates who eschewed violence and wanted a democratic government. Lamartine was a moderate who had carefully courted the left to establish balance. It was he who proclaimed the provisional republican government on February 24.

The government began with a series of compromises between left and right. The crowds outside the Hôtel de Ville, where the deputies met, demanded a socialist republic and called for the red flag to replace France's tricolor. To appease the left, the government promised a living wage to every worker, recognized the rights of labor unions, and set up national workshops to provide government-financed work for the unemployed. Lamartine went along with it all—except for the red flag, which would have signaled a capitulation to the mob.

By March the provisional government had declared universal adult male suffrage and chosen April 9 as the date for an election to establish a new National Assembly. There was massive voter

In this mid-19th-century painting by Millet, *The Gleaners,* a trio of peasant women gather the scattered remains of hay left after harvest. French peasants of the time still farmed with the methods and tools used by their ancestors.

turnout throughout France—84 percent of those eligible to vote. Much to the shock of the leaders of the Revolution, the new assembly was more conservative than moderate, comprising 75 former peers and 439 monarchists but only 231 moderate republicans and 55 radicals. Tocqueville was scornful of the revolutionaries' surprise at the results of the election, knowing they should have held it while the conservatives were still off balance. "There have been more mischievous revolutionaries than those of 1848, but I doubt if there have been any stupider."

Newly eligible peasant voters seemed to be reacting against violence, rising taxes, and government interference, which they attributed to the left-wing republicans. But most of all, the peasants were terrified that their land would be taken away by the socialists. The peasants clung to even the smallest bits of land, which they farmed using methods so primitive that most lived barely at subsistence level. Most farmers still harvested with the sickle rather than with the more efficient scythe in use in England, and yields were low. But the land, in many cases, was all they had.

The new, conservative assembly elected a five-man executive council from which, not surprisingly, socialists were excluded. The result was that hundreds of thousands of workers who had flooded into Paris hoping for employment in the national workshops stormed the assembly in May in an attempt to form a new provisional government. Though they were stopped with the help of the National Guard, discontent and trouble continued to brew.

On May 4, Tocqueville attended a literary luncheon for author George Sand and was surprised to find that she knew a great deal about the workers' organizations. "Try to persuade your friends, sir, not to drive the people into the streets by rousing or offending them," she told him, "for if it comes to a fight . . . you will all perish." He thought she exaggerated the potential for violent opposition but soon discovered his mistake.

On June 21, hoping to disperse the provincial workers, the government closed the national workshops. What followed was close to civil war. But the government was now prepared for insurrection and brutally suppressed the rioters. Three thousand were killed in the streets; 3,000 more were deported to French colonies in Algeria. Then a series of repressive measures were enacted restricting the press and political clubs and meetings. The executive council began to purge radicals from the assembly. The Revolution, in short, was over. Life was back to normal.

On the day that Louis-Philippe had abdicated and Lamartine had stood before the Hôtel de Ville declaring France a republic once again, Tocqueville's thoughts had turned to the many transformations his country had experienced since 1789. France had gone from ancien régime to constitutional monarchy, republic, empire, Restoration, July monarchy, and republic again. "After each of these successive changes it was said that the French Revolution, having achieved what was presumptuously called its work, was finished," he noted. "And here was the French Revolution starting again, for it was always the same one. As we go on, its end seems ever farther off and hazier."

In the years that followed, until his death in 1859, Tocqueville would see the cycle continue. In December 1848 Louis-Napoleon Bonaparte, nephew of Napoleon I, was elected president of the Second Republic for a single, four-year term. Eager to remain in power, he launched a coup d'état three years later to form an authoritarian republic, which extended his term to a decade. Then in December 1852, he took a lesson from his uncle and proclaimed himself emperor of the Second Empire. There was little vocal opposition; many people undoubtedly were afraid of reprisals. But others, their memories perhaps softened by time, saw in this newest emperor a chance to recapture the glory days of their country, when France had been led by a man who seemed to embody the best of the bygone age, of both revolution and Romanticism—Napoleon Bonaparte.

Following the fall of the July monarchy on February 24, 1848, poet and politician Alphonse de Lamartine confronts an angry mob assembled in front of the Hôtel de Ville, Paris's city hall. Lamartine denounced the use of the socialist red "flag of blood" and refused demands to substitute it for France's tricolored emblem, symbol of his nation's unity and strength.

The Age of Napoleon

Astride a noble steed, poised to follow in the footsteps of the world's most courageous men, Napoleon Bonaparte lives on, in history as well as in the painting by David at right, as the embodiment of Romanticism. Napoleon was the quintessential Romantic hero, a larger-than-life leader who started at the bottom and in less than a decade became one of history's greatest statesmen and conquerors. In true Romantic fashion, his amazing success owed less to the circumstances of his time than to his own genius.

Born in Corsica's capital city of Ajaccio in 1769, he was christened Napoleone Buonaparte, a name that reflected his Italian heritage. Both his attorney father Carlo and his mother Letizia supported the doomed Corsican independence movement. "I was born," Napoleon later wrote, "when my country was dying. Thirty thousand Frenchmen disgorged upon our shores, drowning the throne of liberty in a sea of blood; such was the hateful spectacle that offended my infant eyes."

Taking advantage of peace with France, Carlo sent his son off to a French boarding school in 1778. There the shy, melancholy boy was ridiculed for his accent and bullied because of his small stature. He studied hard and received appointments to two elite military academies, where he excelled at everything but the social graces. Commissioned as a second lieutenant at the age of 16, he chose to enter the artillery rather than the more prestigious cavalry because he believed it a faster, less competitive road to advancement.

During the French Revolution, Napoleon bided his time back in Ajaccio. He supported the overthrow of the monarchy, in part because he saw it as an end to French rule in Corsica. But in 1793 local politics forced the entire Buonaparte clan to flee their home and, destitute, they settled in France, changing their name to Bonaparte. With France at war on all its borders, the young officer launched his military career. His first triumph came at the port of Toulon, where his strategically placed guns ended the British siege. Recognized for his tactical brilliance by the ruling Jacobins, he was promoted to brigadier general. He was 24 years old.

The Rise to Power

The year 1796 was noteworthy for young Bonaparte. In March he wed Joséphine de Beauharnais, the pretty widow, courtesan, and jewel of Parisian society with whom he had fallen hopelessly in love. That same month he was named commander in chief of the French army in Italy and embarked on a campaign against northern Italy's Austrian rulers. Napoleon's dazzling victories there enlarged France's realm and treasury and solidified his position as a popular and respected leader of his troops. Two years later, his Egyptian campaign began triumphantly with the defeat of the Turks in the Battle of the Pyramids (far right). Although he eventually abandoned his army to the British and fled Egypt, Napoleon received a hero's welcome on his return in 1799.

Back in Paris, Napoleon joined some of the members of the Directory and Talleyrand in a chaotic coup d'état that forced the ruling Directory to resign. Napoleon seized control of the new three-man Consulate and took the title of First Consul of France. The next few years under his rule were marked by continued military success, financial and domestic stability, improvements in education and the country's infrastructure, and legal reform. The Napoleonic Code would become one of its namesake's greatest and most lasting legacies. By 1802 he held the title First Consul for life, with the right to choose his successor. Napoleon Bonaparte had become, in all but name, France's dictator.

Joséphine de Beauharnais (above) was 33 when she married the 26-year-old Napoleon. Despite her infidelities and extravagant spending habits, he remained devoted, writing, "Whether I am buried in business or leading my troops, my adorable Joséphine fills my mind."

"Citizen Emperor"

"Joseph! If our father could see us!" Napoleon exclaimed excitedly to his older brother as they dressed for the December 2, 1804, coronation in the Cathedral of Notre Dame in Paris. Indeed, the pomp and pageantry of the long-planned event were awe-inspiring. No expense had been spared on readying the cathedral—preparations included the removal of a number of homes around it to facilitate the ceremonial procession—nor on the jewels, clothing, and other regalia worn by the members of the court.

The emperor-to-be was himself resplendent in robes of embroidered velvet, ermine, satin, and lace. He wore an antique wreath of gold laurel leaves crowning his brow and carried a scepter reputed to have belonged to Charlemagne in his hand *(right)*. Joséphine, ablaze with diamonds and, according to one witness, looking no older than 25, wobbled under the weight of her 80-pound velvet and ermine train. Only the grudging assistance of her husband's envious sisters prevented her from falling backward as she approached the altar of the cathedral *(far right)*.

Napoleon had invited Pope Pius VII to officiate at his coronation. However, he was not invited to crown him—that would have subjected the emperor to the authority of the church, something he could not allow. Instead, after Pius finished blessing the two crowns, Napoleon slowly and deliberately faced the congregation and placed the larger of the two on his own head. He then crowned the kneeling and tearful Joséphine with the smaller one. *"Vivat Imperator in aeternum!"* intoned the compliant pontiff. Napoleon Bonaparte was France's emperor. Now all he needed was an heir.

Success and a Son

The years immediately following Napoleon's coronation were a heady time for all the Bonapartes. France's domination of Europe became a family affair as the emperor placed three of his brothers, one brother-in-law, one sister, and his stepson on the thrones of various countries, duchies, and principalities. On the battlefield, Napoleon's string of successes continued, including the Battle of Austerlitz in 1805, often considered his masterpiece as a military strategist. By 1810 most of the European continent west of Russia was either directly or indirectly part of Napoleon's Empire of the French.

Still, there was no son to inherit the vast realm and ensure its stability and permanence. Because he had fathered at least two illegitimate children by mistresses, Napoleon came to the conclusion that Joséphine was to blame for their infertility. He reluctantly divorced his beloved wife in 1809, after tearfully promising her, "I will always be your friend."

The following year the emperor married the plump, naive, and plain 18-year-old Archduchess Marie-Louise of Austria both for political reasons and because her family had a history of remarkable fertility. In 1811 his choice paid off—Marie-Louise gave birth to Napoleon II *(below)*, on whom his delighted father promptly bestowed the grand title of King of Rome.

At the head of his general staff and 20,000 horse grenadiers, Napoleon triumphantly enters Berlin through its Brandenburg Gate in October 1806 *(far right)*. After his victories at Jena and Auerstädt, he had written, "The Prussian army no longer exists."

Napoleon's Last Battles

Napoleon's downfall was nearly as swift as his rise. Starting with a lengthy, ill-fated military intervention in Spain and continuing through the catastrophic Russian campaign in 1812, France's power in Europe eroded. By March 1814 a coalition of allied nations occupied Paris. Napoleon abdicated and accepted banishment to the island of Elba, off Italy's northwest coast, where he immediately began to plot his return to France.

Napoleon seemed to have made a successful comeback in March 1815, but his second reign ended in June with total defeat at Waterloo. This time the allies chose a more remote place of exile—the South Atlantic island of St. Helena. For the next six years, the former emperor lived quietly on this tiny outpost, dictating the memoirs that would fuel the heroic legacy he was certain would be his. As usual, his confidence was justified—but he did not live to see it. He died on St. Helena on May 5, 1821.

Napoleon gazes from the deck of a British warship taking him to St. Helena *(far right)*. His spirits rose during the voyage when he began his memoirs. "My destiny is the opposite of other men's," he wrote. "Other men are lowered by their downfall, my own raises me to infinite heights. I shall survive!" Indeed, 20 years after his death, the emperor's remains were returned in triumph to Paris for interment *(below)*.

CHAPTER TWO

Symphonies and Fairy Tales

Ludwig van Beethoven *(left)* is portrayed composing the *Missa Solemnis,* considered one of his masterpieces. Beethoven, famous for his artistic temperament as well as his genius, lived and worked in the glittering city of Vienna, where people from all over Europe flocked to hear music, attend the theater, and participate in the chic salons.

 One late spring day in 1804, when the horse chestnuts blossomed in every Viennese square, 20-year-old Ferdinand Ries, bursting with news, climbed the long flights of stairs that led to the apartment of Ludwig van Beethoven. A mentor and friend, Beethoven not only taught Ries, a brilliant young musician, but had helped support him since Ries appeared penniless in the city, driven from their native Bonn by French invaders. After three years of companionship, Ries was confident that his news justified interrupting the often-irascible composer's work.

The apartment Ries entered at last was a treasure-filled wreck. The furniture was crude and damaged; old food lay moldering on chair seats. On the other hand, there were endless shelves of books, from the *Iliad,* the *Odyssey,* and a host of other Greek and Roman works to complete editions of German poets such as Johann von Goethe, Friedrich von Schiller, and Johann von Herder, not to mention a well-thumbed and annotated volume of Shakespeare, beloved by German Romantics (they thought his verse even better in their language). There were also matchless musical instruments presented to Beethoven by his noble patrons, including several pianos as well as violins and violoncellos created by such masters as Guarneri and Amati. And piled in a corner, jealously guarded, were Beethoven's own scratched and blotted musical scores. Ries, whose studies included making copies of the works, was familiar with most of them, including the mighty Third Symphony, completed early that spring but not yet performed.

Surprising as it might seem, considering the humiliating treaties recently imposed on Austria by France, this symphony was dedicated to Napoleon Bonaparte. Yet Beethoven was hardly alone in his Napoleonic sympathies. German and Austrian philosophers and artists, such as Kant and Schiller, who had seen the French Revolution as a leap forward for human freedom, believed Bonaparte to be its embodiment. Goethe kept a bust of the First Consul in his study. Like those men, Beethoven envisioned Bonaparte as a hero, the very figure of the enlightened leader.

Ries's news would destroy that vision. The First Consul, he told Beethoven, had declared himself emperor of the French on May 28. The composer exploded in a characteristic rage: The dark eyes flashed under their heavy brows, the swarthy, pock-marked skin reddened, the hairy hands flailed as he shouted of Napoleon's perfidy. "Is he, then, too, nothing more than an ordinary human being?" Beethoven cried with dismay. "Now he, too, will trample on all the rights of man and indulge only his ambition. He will exalt himself above all others, become a tyrant!" Then, as Ries later recalled, Beethoven snatched the Third Symphony from the table where it lay, "took hold of the title page by the top, tore it in two, and threw it on the floor."

The sense of betrayal had its echoes among all those who had believed in the French Revolution and in Napoleon Bonaparte. But Beethoven's feelings were more complex and ambiguous than his angry gesture indicated. Even several months later, he was

Residents of late-18th-century Vienna drive, stroll, work, and gossip on one of the main avenues, the Graben, a street filled with elegant shops and ornate fountains. The city's population in 1792, when Beethoven arrived, was 20 times that of Bonn, his previous home.

still considering dedicating the great symphony to the new emperor. Indeed, the symphony, with its hammering opening chords, its majestic second movement, its grieving themes that are resolved in a vision of supreme beauty, was of a grand scale that fit the image of Napoleon, that colossus bestriding all of Europe. When the score was published, it was named the *Eroica*—the heroic symphony. Beethoven dedicated it to Prince Franz Joseph Lobkowitz, who was one of his patrons, but he added to the title page the enigmatic words, "to celebrate the memory of a great man."

Publication of the Third Symphony ushered in an era filled with the intensely personal music that characterized Romanticism. Ludwig van Beethoven himself was the paradigm of the artist-hero, whose genius allows him to recognize and shape new expressions of the spiritual essence underlying the material world and, in doing so, to triumphantly transcend earthly sorrow. Beethoven explored what German painter Caspar David Friedrich called "the only source of true art . . . our own heart," and in his search found truth that he conveyed in what the Romantics saw as the purest of mediums, music. Beethoven's work, wrote fellow composer and music critic E. T. A. Hoffmann, "opens the floodgates of fear, of terror, of horror, of pain, and aroused that longing for the eternal which is the essence of romanticism."

In a sense, the music offered hope and order in the midst of fragmented reality—and few realities were as

fragmented as that of the German states during Beethoven's lifetime. When the composer was born in 1770, the tattered, 700-year-old Holy Roman Empire still loosely united 300 German states, ranging from tiny duchies to the muscle-flexing kingdom of Prussia in the north and the vast and polyglot Austrian Empire in the south. Sixty-three of these states were ruled by churchmen; 51 were free cities such as Hamburg. Some states were Protestant, others Roman Catholic. The highest aristocrats among them—and few regions were so class ridden as this—chose an emperor, generally an Austrian Habsburg, from among their own ranks. The purpose of government was to maintain the status quo and dynastic power.

By the time Beethoven was 19, at the dawn of the French Revolution in 1789, that world was on the verge of dissolution, although few could have foreseen it. During the next decades, the map would be repeatedly rearranged by Bonaparte's armies; the German states would suffer humiliating defeat after defeat, powerless to stop the French invaders. Vienna itself would be occupied twice. In 1806, Napoleon's military victories would bring an end to the Holy Roman Empire. When France finally was vanquished and Napoleon permanently exiled nine years later, the German Confederation, a loose organization of the German states, was formed. Most political power remained with the individual states, however.

Yet throughout this troubled period,

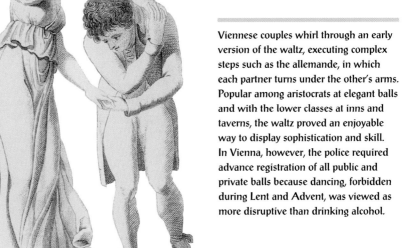

Viennese couples whirl through an early version of the waltz, executing complex steps such as the allemande, in which each partner turns under the other's arms. Popular among aristocrats at elegant balls and with the lower classes at inns and taverns, the waltz proved an enjoyable way to display sophistication and skill. In Vienna, however, the police required advance registration of all public and private balls because dancing, forbidden during Lent and Advent, was viewed as more disruptive than drinking alcohol.

the Austrian capital nourished a sparkling intellectual and artistic life, with music—already its most famed art—at the center. Revolutionary energies poured out as artistic innovation. Ludwig van Beethoven, who would spend most of his life in Vienna, both embodied and mirrored the changing world. During Beethoven's early years in the city, the salon, a regular, informal gathering usually hosted by a woman, remained a central feature of aristocratic and intellectual life. The custom had come, like so many others, from France. Unlike the salons of the Parisian writer Germaine de Staël, Viennese salons were not usually openly political, such activities being imprudent in a police state such as Austria. Instead, they revolved around the arts, especially music. They were the only places in that rigidly stratified society where the first (hereditary) and second (appointed) ranks of the nobility mingled socially with the middle classes and with artists. The cosmopolitan nature of the Viennese salons was exemplified by one of the city's most famous *salonnières,* Fanny von Arnstein, who on the surface appeared unlikely to succeed in Viennese society. She was of the second rank, a Prussian (who were often regarded suspiciously by the Austrians), and a Jew—in a city with a long history of anti-Semitism and a stern set of anti-Semitic laws. Yet her salon flourished.

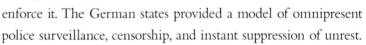

Arnstein and Beethoven both would reach the apogee of their public lives during the glittering Congress of Vienna of 1814-1815. The business of its representatives, who included most of Europe's rulers, was to reorder Europe's political structure following the long-delayed downfall of Napoleon's empire and to establish a balance of European powers. But attending parties and concerts and having love affairs seemed to be just as important to the attendees.

The architects of the new balance of power insisted that *Ruhe und Ordnung*—"tranquillity and order"—should distinguish Europe in the post-Napoleonic era and encouraged all governments to enforce it. The German states provided a model of omnipresent police surveillance, censorship, and instant suppression of unrest.

In the midst of this political oppression, the rising middle class engendered a new period of domestic stability centered on the simple pleasures of home, family, reading, and delight in the outdoors. This time would be known as the Biedermeier age, signifying a modest and delightful style in painting, furniture, poetry, and even music. It was in many ways a reaction against the political upheavals of the preceding decades and the wild emotion of the Romantic way of thinking.

An important aspect of the Biedermeier age was a newfound pride in all things German and a nationalistic movement toward the establishment of a united Germany. During this period serious studies of the German language and folklore would be undertaken. Among the great philological scholars were the brothers Grimm, Jacob and Wilhelm. But the comfortable Biedermeier period would come to an explosive end in 1848. Political oppression and economic hardship would send the flames of revolution racing across the German states.

Beethoven, who would die in 1827, would not be witness to the vast cultural changes that took place in the second quarter of the century. But the amazing music that he would leave behind would continue to be heard and admired long after the cries of the 1848 revolutionaries had died away.

Ludwig van Beethoven was born into a family of court musicians that served the Elector of Cologne, a princely archbishop whose seat was in Bonn. Court orchestras were an intrinsic part of life in the scores of principalities of the Holy Roman Empire. They produced masses, cantatas, and oratorios for princely chapels, and operas, ballets, and orchestral works for royal entertainments. The musicians were servants, salaried and liveried and—when they performed well—tipped.

Ludwig's Flemish grandfather and namesake had been Kapellmeister, or musical director, for an Elector of Cologne. His father, Johann, less talented and certainly less disciplined, sang in the Elector's choir; he was also an alcoholic. Ludwig's mother bore eight children, watched five die, and viewed marriage as "a chain of sorrows." By the time Ludwig was four or five, Johann, having recognized the boy's gifts, had him at the harpsichord, hoping no doubt to develop the kind of profitable prodigy that Leopold Mozart had made of his son Wolfgang.

Johann van Beethoven was no Leopold Mozart. His musical skills were mediocre, and he was, it was widely reported, a cruel teacher who kept his tiny son weeping at his work at all hours. Fortunately, within a few years, as his gift became obvious, the boy attracted better mentors. By the time he was 12, Ludwig was harpsichordist for the Elector's orchestra; a few years later he was second organist, with a salary and a uniform of sea-green dress coat, green knee breeches, and silk stockings.

Beethoven worked in the vast electoral palace, a French-Italianate affair extravagantly adorned with gilt furniture, glittering chandeliers, and huge mirrors. Its gardens were magnificent in the classically ordered style of Versailles. It had its own concert hall and, underneath, its own theater.

Goethe's Masterpiece

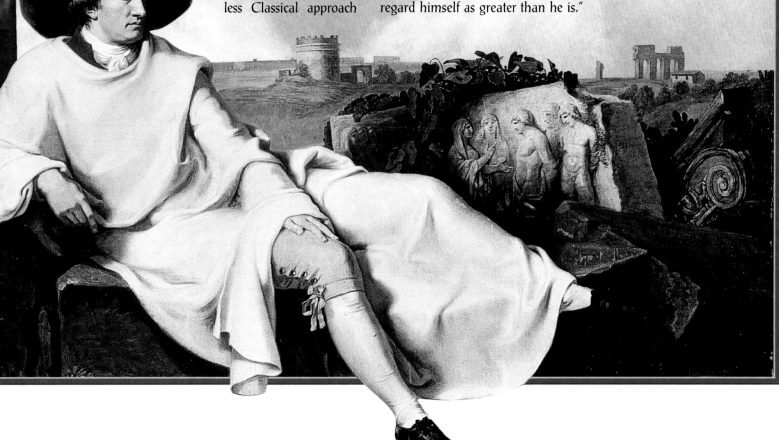

Despairing at the waste of his life, an aging scholar flings open a magic book and rashly summons a spirit to his aid. Flames explode above him and a terrifying apparition appears *(left)*. The man tries to banish it but is persuaded to make a bargain instead: He will receive renewed youth and momentary happiness in exchange for his soul.

Thus begins the epic drama *Faust,* written by Johann Wolfgang von Goethe. The writer was born in 1749 in Frankfurt am Main, son of a middle-class lawyer. As a university student, Goethe developed an interest in the occult and in folk tales, poetry, and Shakespeare, all of which inspired him to take a more naturalistic and less Classical approach in his writing. His early poems, plays, and novels established him as the central figure of the late-18th-century Sturm und Drang (storm and stress) literary movement, which rejected the rationalism of the Enlightenment and advocated an intense emotionalism.

In 1775, Goethe became a court adviser to the Saxe-Weimar duchy, but he continued to write. In 1786, he traveled to Italy *(below)* to renew his spirit and gained a greater appreciation for Classical art forms. When he returned to Weimar, he resumed work on *Faust,* begun in the 1770s but not completed until 1831, a year before his death.

The most celebrated intellectual of his day, Goethe, unlike Faust, made his own success, based on a simple philosophy: "For a man to achieve all that is demanded of him, he must regard himself as greater than he is."

For the boy, this was the right place and the right time. The Electors had all been devoted to music, and the man who succeeded to the throne in 1784, Maximilian Franz, brother of the Habsburg emperor, was particularly enthusiastic about it. The palace boasted a huge music library and constant performances—operas by Mozart, Domenico Cimarosa, Antonio Salieri, and the incomparable Christoph Gluck; and orchestral pieces by many others, among them Mozart and Franz Joseph Haydn, who were both then working in Vienna.

At the palace, with all the world's music for inspiration and with skilled teachers, Beethoven blossomed. He mastered most orchestral instruments—strings, wind, brass—and his keyboard skills were astonishing. In an age that valued keyboard improvisation, he was a virtuoso. His talent and his shy, rough personality earned him the affection of Bonn courtiers, among them the von Breuning family, who welcomed him as part of the household. This was unusual enough, in a society where class lines were so jealously drawn that aristocratic litigants used different courts than did other classes and university students of noble birth sat separately from commoners. Yet the von Breunings were only the first of many noble patrons who took Beethoven under their wing.

Other musicians saw young Beethoven's potential as well. The boy had a trip to Vienna in 1787 (though it was cut short by the illness of his mother, who died soon after his return home). There he played improvisations for Mozart. "Keep your eyes on him," Mozart informed his friends. "Someday he will give the world something to talk about."

When Haydn passed through Bonn, returning from a triumphant British tour, he examined a cantata Beethoven had written and agreed to accept him as a pupil in composition. Franz Joseph Haydn was Austria's greatest living master, and he was Kapellmeister for Prince

Fashionable 19th-century Viennese ride in luxuriously appointed horse-drawn carriages, while other city dwellers stroll about the treelined grounds or sit at tables outside the coffeehouse in the Prater, a well-known park and gathering place.

Miklós Esterházy in Eisenstadt for almost 30 years. Most court musicians were merely competent craftsmen, but Haydn, like Johann Sebastian Bach of the generation before, was a brilliant exception. He valued his court position in part for the freedom for innovation it offered him.

In early November 1792, with a small stipend from Maximilian Franz and the good wishes of friends and patrons, Beethoven left Bonn, never to return. The road to Vienna ran along the Danube River, through a landscape of forest, fields, and villages, of towering cliffs crowned with fortresses and monasteries. It passed through the enchanting Vienna Woods and through a gate in the wall that protected the suburban villages surrounding Vienna, then crossed an open, sloping area called the Glacis, once a moat guarding the city's great wall. Built as a defense against Turkish invaders, this wall was so huge and thick that the top served as a promenade in fine weather.

Within the wall lay a city of twisting streets and towering spires, churches and palaces. Its heart—and the heart of the Holy Roman Empire—was the Hofburg, a vast imperial complex that included damp and crumbling 15th-century palaces as well as magnificent, light-filled baroque ones with damasked walls and painted ceilings. The complex also included a great Imperial Library and the famed Spanish Riding School, where the white horses known as Lippizaners were trained. All around lay the palaces of the nobility. In narrower streets stood apartment buildings of all sorts, grand mansions cheek by jowl with tenements.

The city housed 200,000 people, who were famous for their frivolity, for a peculiar insouciant spirit masking the deeper sadnesses of their difficult age. They were also famous for their love of food. "A well-to-do citizen in Vienna is eating almost at every moment of the day," wrote an austere Prussian in disapproval.

The Viennese were even more famed for their devotion to theater and music. The city boasted two court theaters, where operas and ballets were performed. There also were innumerable private concerts in the mansions of the aristocracy, public concerts to celebrate national and religious holidays, and public recitals known as academies for visiting performers. There were ballrooms and music halls for dancing. In the streets and squares, among puppeteers, jugglers, magicians, animal acts, and sausage vendors, one could hear musicians of every kind. Publishers' shops featured musical scores. Even the poor ornamented their open windows with caged birds—canaries, finches, nightingales—whose songs echoed in the streets.

With the help of assiduous labor you will receive Mozart's spirit from Haydn's hand," wrote an early patron, Count Ferdinand von Waldstein, in Beethoven's Bonn farewell book, signed by his patrons and friends. Indeed, thanks to Waldstein's and Maximilian Franz's letters of introduction, Haydn's interest, and Beethoven's own tremendous authority at the keyboard, the newcomer to Vienna was recognized immediately as a rare talent. Haydn taught him counterpoint; Johann Georg Albrechtsberger, Kapellmeister of the famed St. Stephen's church, took him through orchestral exercises; Antonio Salieri, the imperial Kapellmeister, once Mozart's rival and rumored (wrongly, Beethoven thought) to be his murderer, instructed him in writing for voice.

The nobility of Vienna, a cosmopolitan mixture of great names from all over the empire—Italy, Hungary, the Balkan states, Prussia—lionized him. Their patronage and protection were crucial: All arts and most business in Austria depended on the ruling class.

Initially, Beethoven found a cheap room to live in. It was, he wrote, "miserable," but he did not suffer for long. Within weeks he was living in one of Vienna's more splendid palaces, owned by Prince Karl and Princess Christiane Lichnowsky. Like the von Breunings before them, the prince and princess came to view Beethoven almost as a son. They were not much older than he, but they were nobility, fabulously rich from landholdings in Silesia,

An animal trainer puts a trained dog through its paces at a fairground in the city of Munich. Men, women, and children of all classes gawk at the strange sights, which include a monkey chattering atop a camel and a pack of fancifully costumed canines *(right)*. Animal shows like this one were the forerunners of the modern circus.

During a scene from the 19th-century play *1722, 1822, 1922*, actors gesture and declaim to a full house in the Theater in der Josefstadt, in a Viennese suburb. Like other popular comedies of the late 18th and early 19th centuries, this piece by prolific playwright Karl Meisl was not fully scripted, offering the players plenty of opportunities for improvisation.

famed for their love and support of music, and impeccably connected.

Prince Karl, a serious pianist, had been a friend and pupil of Mozart's; the princess, so lovely that she was called one of Vienna's "Three Graces," was the daughter of famous music patrons and a fine musician in her own right. Her sister was married to another eminent devotee of music, the Russian ambassador Count Andreas Razumovsky. The count was an expert violinist who had learned to play Haydn's difficult quartets from the master himself; eventually Razumovsky would create a distinguished private quartet, to whom he gave lifetime contracts.

Among others in this musical circle were Baron Gottfried van Swieten, director of the Imperial Library, who organized a society for the preservation of the choral music of

George Frideric Handel and Johann Sebastian Bach (then little appreciated) and who had written the librettos for Haydn's oratorios, *The Seasons* and *The Creation*. There were also Prince Franz Joseph Lobkowitz, described as being as "good hearted as a child and the greatest fool for music one can imagine"; Count Nikolaus von Domanovecz, secretary of the Hungarian Chancellery, who devoted himself to the composer; and the widely traveled Count Moritz von Fries, to whom Beethoven dedicated several compositions.

These people lived lives of almost unimaginable privilege and sometimes remarkable decadence. Lobkowitz had a passion for solitude: He would spend weeks in seclusion, observing passersby in a huge mirror installed in his apartment so that he could see without being seen; he would leave mail unopened for years. Razumovsky had cut a wide swath through the ranks of the

Recognizing in Beethoven something new, his patrons were tolerant of his many eccentricities. He had left the courtly style behind in Bonn. A pianist of the time gave a little picture of the composer, a portent of a changing world. "I remember very well," the musician wrote, "how Haydn as well as Salieri sat in the small music-room on a side-sofa, both of them most carefully dressed in the older fashion, with a chignon, shoes and silk stockings, while Beethoven used to appear in the Rhenish fashion, freer, not to say carelessly dressed."

In fact, Beethoven's dress was variable in his youth, ranging from derelict to dapper depending on his mood. His feelings about family and class were just as mixed. Coming as he did from a miserably unhappy house, he longed for family life: The Lichnowskys were one of his many substitute families. Even when he

"He knew how to produce such an effect upon every hearer that frequently not an eye remained dry."

ladies of Europe during his diplomatic career: The queen of Naples was one of his more notorious conquests. Karl Lichnowsky was known as a "cynical lecher," his behavior infamous even in licentious Vienna, where the 11:30 service at one fashionable church was called the "whores' mass" because of the crowds of late-rising prostitutes who attended.

When it came to musicians, though, the Viennese aristocrats' attention turned gallant and supportive. The Lichnowskys gave regular Friday morning concerts; the others arranged concerts and recitals as well and saw to it that their young protégé's genius received imperial attention—and financial rewards, including regular stipends.

moved away to live in a succession of apartments on his own, he tried to stay near them. But he also chafed at the bonds: "They treated me like a grandson," he would say. "The princess's affection became at times so oversolicitous that she would have made a glass shade to put over me, so that no unworthy person might touch or breathe upon me."

Beethoven wanted to be seen as equal to his noble benefactors. Although his accent and manners made it obvious he was a commoner, he did not deny the misconception that the Flemish "van" of his name was actually a German "von," signifying gentle birth; he left unchallenged for years the rumor that he was the illegitimate son of the king of Prussia.

The composer was inordinately sensitive to anything that could be construed as patronizing. Prince Lichnowsky, ever thoughtful, once directed his servant to answer Beethoven's bell first if both their bells rang at once; Beethoven immediately engaged his own servant. When the composer was learning to ride, the prince offered the freedom of his stables; Beethoven bought his own horse, then forgot about it. He objected to the grand dinners the Lichnowskys gave at 4 p.m. each day, with bells rung three times to announce a prince and twice for a count. "Am I supposed to come home every day at half-past three, change my clothes, shave, and all that?" he asked, and went off to eat in a tavern.

Beethoven was capable of great affection and kindness and loved a joke, but he had a terrible temper. He quarreled with his patrons, with his teachers, with his friends; his rages were sudden and often violent. He was known to throw food at waiters. Usually his scenes would be followed by extreme penitence; he seemed to want in the most idealistic way to be a good man.

Generally his friends and patrons stuck with him. Much was forgiven because of the magnetism of his nature and because people realized his greatness early. They first knew him as a pianist in a new style that some found rough compared with the delicacy of most keyboard virtuosos. It had enormous power over audiences, and a contemporary remarked, "In whatever company he might chance to be, he knew how to produce such an effect upon every hearer that frequently not an eye remained dry, while many would break out into loud sobs; for there was something wonderful in his expression in addition to the beauty and originality of his ideas and his spirited style of rendering them."

Within only a few years, his fame as a composer had grown and publishers were waiting for his works. His patrons did all they could to help him: Lichnowsky studied and played the difficult piano sonatas to assure Beethoven that they could be executed by someone other than a virtuoso. Razumovsky put his private quartet at Beethoven's disposal: "He was as much at home in Razumovsky's palace as a hen in her coop," an observer commented. "Everything he wrote was taken warm from the nest and tried out in the frying pan. Every note was played precisely as he wanted it played, with such devotion, such love, such obedience, such piety as could be inspired only by a passionate admiration of his great genius." Because Beethoven was notoriously clumsy—his pockmarked face was always decorated with shaving cuts—Nikolaus von Domanovecz cut all the composer's quill pens for him, to prevent damage to his precious hands.

To make a living Beethoven also had to be an entrepreneur. He accepted some pupils,

Strollers enjoy the luxurious gardens surrounding the palatial home in Vienna of Count Andreas Razumovsky, shown at right with the plans for the spectacular house and grounds. Beethoven, an honored guest, frequently attended concerts at Razumovsky Palace before it burned down in 1814.

including the Habsburg archduke Rudolf, brother of the emperor, whom he treated firmly. He performed in noble houses, where he was discreetly paid by a member of the staff, the money presented in an elegant little box. He hawked regional rights to his compositions to publishers who sold the scores at retail. He persuaded patrons to purchase new works, which he dedicated to them. He performed his own work at benefit concerts, for which he hired the hall, paid performance taxes, performed, conducted, and even sold the tickets. All of these activities proved tiresome.

Relief from the necessity of pursuing these avenues of income arrived in 1809 after Beethoven received an invitation from King Jérôme of Westphalia (brother of Napoleon) to join his new court as Kapellmeister. The possibility that Ludwig van Beethoven might leave Vienna inspired three patrons to provide him with a comfortable salary for the rest of his life, provided he stayed in Vienna or at least in Austria; they promised he would be left undisturbed for "the invention of works of magnitude."

This generous support freed Beethoven for the great efforts of composition that since the turn of the century had pervaded his whole being. He lived in a world of music, rising, breakfasting, and going directly to his desk to compose. In the afternoons he walked tirelessly, carrying his notebook so that he could sketch out ideas at any moment. Every summer he stayed among the mountains and meadows of the Austrian countryside, first at the country houses of his patrons, then at various rented rooms. He walked and walked, absorbed and inspired, Rousseau-like, by nature: He wrote, "Every tree said to me, 'Holy! Holy!'"

These reveries far from the city were crucial to the explosion of creativity and innovation of Beethoven's early 30s. Certainly the flood of Romantic thought, especially German Romantic thought, aroused currents in his mind. His formal education outside music was rudimentary: His spelling was atrocious, and his math was restricted to simple addition. Yet Beethoven read with

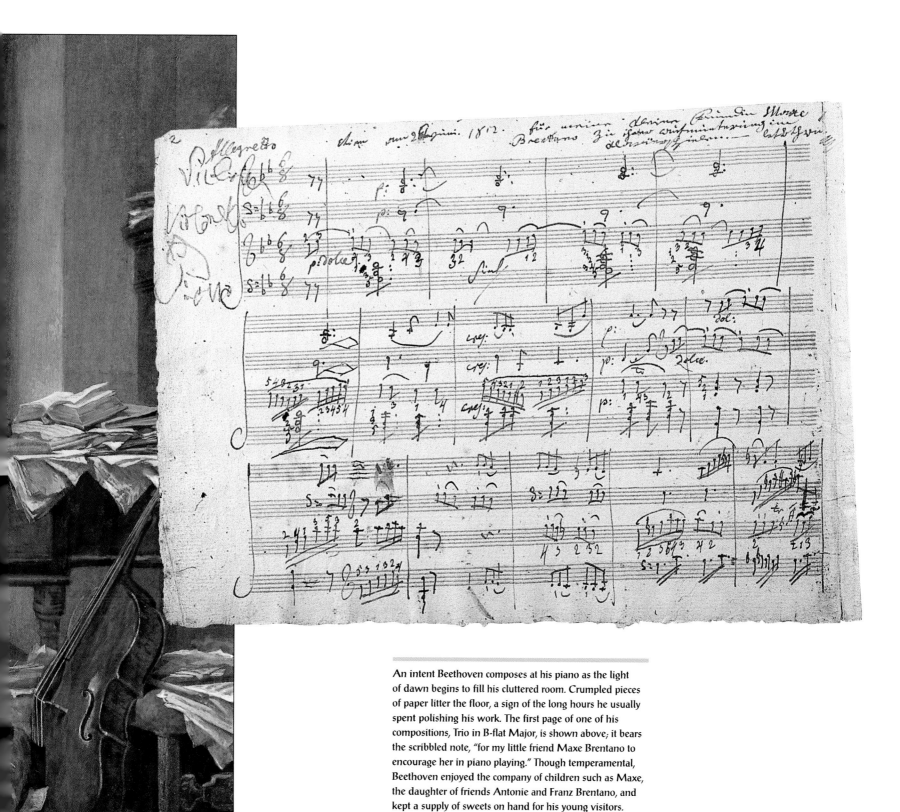

An intent Beethoven composes at his piano as the light of dawn begins to fill his cluttered room. Crumpled pieces of paper litter the floor, a sign of the long hours he usually spent polishing his work. The first page of one of his compositions, Trio in B-flat Major, is shown above; it bears the scribbled note, "for my little friend Maxe Brentano to encourage her in piano playing." Though temperamental, Beethoven enjoyed the company of children such as Maxe, the daughter of friends Antonie and Franz Brentano, and kept a supply of sweets on hand for his young visitors.

obsessive intensity. He deeply admired and often quoted the plays of Friedrich von Schiller; years later, the writer's great "Ode to Joy" would provide the heart of Beethoven's sublime final symphony. His attitude toward Goethe amounted to hero worship. From them, from others, and from deep within himself, he learned to explore the Romantics' vision of pitiless fate, to trust the creative forces of acceptance and love, and to believe in the central role of the artist in revealing these eternal realities.

The composer yearned for love and sought it repeatedly. The women he admired were young, musical, beautiful, aristocratic, and unattainable— because of their rank, because he was uncouth, because they were married. The names of those rumored to be his lovers echo in his dedications and in scattered notes: Countess Giulietta Guicciardi, to whom he dedicated the *Moonlight Sonata;* Josephine von Brunsvik, the unhappily married Countess von Deym, whom he called "the angel of my heart" and for whom he wrote the song *To Hope;* the invalid Countess Maria Erdödy, for whom he wrote a happy trio in E-flat major and the mysterious D major *Ghost Trio.*

These and other women revered his genius—but rejected his person; only one woman, it seems, returned his love. The first indication of her existence would appear after his death, when friends found in a drawer the missive known as the "Immortal Beloved" letter. Never mailed, the letter was written in the summer of 1812, when Beethoven was staying at the Bohemian resort of Teplitz and the woman at Karlsbad. Her love, he wrote, made him the "happiest and unhappiest of men," but union was impossible. "Why this deep sorrow when necessity speaks. . . . Can you change the fact that you are not wholly mine, I not wholly thine?" The letter, written over a period of two days, was signed, "ever thine, ever mine, ever ours."

The woman's name was not revealed in the letter, but people almost immediately began speculating about her identity. Some thought she may have been Antonie

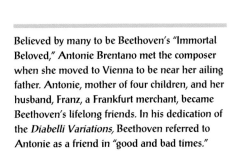

Believed by many to be Beethoven's "Immortal Beloved," Antonie Brentano met the composer when she moved to Vienna to be near her ailing father. Antonie, mother of four children, and her husband, Franz, a Frankfurt merchant, became Beethoven's lifelong friends. In his dedication of the *Diabelli Variations,* Beethoven referred to Antonie as a friend in "good and bad times."

Some people think Josephine von Brunsvik, not Brentano, was Beethoven's mysterious love. During Brunsvik's first impoverished and unhappy marriage, he offered her free piano lessons. After she was widowed, Beethoven courted her, writing 13 love letters. She rejected him, then wed someone else. That union proved as cheerless as her first and ended in separation.

Brentano, an aristocratic Viennese statesman's daughter married to a kind Frankfurt merchant. In 1812 she was 32 and had four children. Beethoven had become friendly with the entire family two years earlier, during the Brentanos' extended stay in Antonie's beloved Vienna. Antonie Brentano worshiped the composer's genius and then came to love him. Her affections were obviously returned. When she became reclusive, grieving at the thought of the family's return to Frankfurt, which she hated, Beethoven would come to her. As a friend of Brentano's related, the composer would "seat himself at the pianoforte in her anteroom without a word, and improvise . . . [then] he would go as he had come, without taking notice of another person." The composer immortalized Brentano in the dedication to the *Diabelli Variations.*

But during these years more than a failed love affair was driving Beethoven implacably toward solitude: loss of hearing. Its effects began in his late 20s. Though his deafness to conversation did not become profound until 1812 and to music until 1817, it began to isolate him immediately. In 1801, he wrote a friend, "my ears continue to hum and buzz day and night. I must confess that I lead a miserable life. For almost two years I have ceased to attend any social function. . . . If I had any other profession I might be able to cope with my infirmity."

Beethoven rushed from doctor to doctor, hoping to find a cure. The medicine of the age, however, could not even cope with known endemic diseases—cholera, typhus, typhoid, smallpox, syphilis—let alone the composer's mysterious malady.

At first, Beethoven despaired and entertained thoughts of suicide. Ferdinand Ries, who visited the composer in the country village of Heiligenstadt twice between 1800 and 1802, wrote, "I called his attention to a shepherd who was piping very agreeably in the woods on a flute made of a twig of elder. For half an hour Beethoven could hear nothing . . . he became extremely quiet and morose."

In the summer of 1802, 31-year-old Beethoven *(right)* spent many hours wandering through the small rustic village of Heiligenstadt *(below),* a suburb of Vienna, creating new music as always but also coming to terms with his advancing deafness. To hide his hearing loss, Beethoven avoided social gatherings, explaining in a letter written from Heiligenstadt, "How could I possibly admit an infirmity in the *one sense* which ought to be more perfect in me than in others." While staying in the village, he overcame his thoughts of suicide and made the courageous resolution to accept the challenge of his deafness by embarking on a new creative path.

But somehow the composer found the courage to go on and pursue his music. "Every day brings me nearer to the goal which I feel but cannot describe," he wrote. "I will seize fate by the throat; it shall certainly not bend and crush me completely."

And heroically, from this crucible of lost loves, aural isolation, a country at war, and a city twice invaded, he forged matchless music. Before 1800 he had produced marvelous works, some of them masterpieces, but on the smaller scale of chamber music. Now works on a grand scale poured out: an opera, an oratorio, a mass, six symphonies, four concertos, five string quartets, three trios, three string sonatas, six piano sonatas, not to mention music for the stage, lieder, piano variations, and several symphonic overtures.

With these works Beethoven revolutionized music. Without leaving the classical sonata form that, with its three or four movements (exposition, development, recapitulation, coda), is the basis of symphonic music, he expanded it to previously unimagined size. Into its structure he introduced complexities, asymmetries, atonalities, and powerful, overarching harmonies that transformed his works into dramas of the human soul. Every emotion, from the lightest to the most terrifying, was organically incorporated, allowed to conflict, and transcended within the music itself. It was the music of mortality— and of the renewal of life.

There was some resistance, especially among older musicians, to his wrenching style, but generally speaking, Beethoven fever swept Europe. By 1808 his name on a concert program anywhere in the Habsburg lands ensured success; he was enormously popular in England. Only French musicians avoided his compositions. Having evolved like many of his countrymen into a Francophobe, he merely observed that "the French find my music beyond their powers of performance."

In the second decade of the century, the shadows began to close around the composer. His annuity shrank in worth by four-fifths due to heavy war indemnities from France that forced a devaluation of the currency. His patrons began to die or, like Razumovsky, return to their own countries.

It was Razumovsky, however, along with Archduke Rudolf, who saw that Beethoven was rewarded well enough to support him for the rest of his days by staging a gala concert for his benefit during the Congress of Vienna. The congress officially began on October 1, 1814, after Napoleon's defeat and exile to Elba.

Europe had never seen anything to compare with this congress. Some 100,000 foreigners flooded into the city beginning in September 1814, among them the czar of Russia, four kings, five princes, innumerable dukes and archdukes, and many lesser notables, all with vast retinues. Everyone wanted something from it: dispossessed princes their land restored, larger states additional territory, dispossessed peoples their rights returned. Above all that, people wanted some assurance that the horrors of the last 20 years would not be repeated.

Their relief at victory after years of defeat and their pride as hosts to the meeting produced a special gaiety in the Viennese. The organization (and costs) fell to the Austrian emperor Francis I; his delicate, tubercular young wife, Maria Ludovica; and their staff. It was Maria and Prince Trauttmansdorff, marshal of the court and master of the horse, who commanded the Festivals Committee. They had to organize everything from meals and accommodations to entertainment and transportation.

Forty tables were set for dinner every night in the Hofburg, where many of the distinguished guests were staying. To eliminate precedence problems among the pack of royals, the guests were ranked by age. This meant the empress as hostess had as her constant dinner partner the elderly king of Württemberg, so fat a half-moon had to be cut out of the table to allow him to belly up.

Besides dinners, there was a ball at the Hofburg every week, as well as royal receptions on Mondays and Saturdays. There were shooting parties at imperial country estates. And there were many even more extravagant affairs. The congress opened with a victory parade of the Austrian army through the lines of chestnut trees of the promenade in the Prater, a park located on a charming pleasure island in the Danube. This was followed by a Peace Ball for 1,800. There was a brilliantly executed medieval tournament in the Hofsburg's riding hall.

Trauttmansdorff provided 300 gleaming carriages varnished green and adorned with the imperial arms in yellow, 1,400 horses, and the necessary coachmen and grooms to transport the eminent guests. When the unusually mild weather finally turned snowy in January, guests were taken from the city in a convoy of brightly painted sleighs (accompanied by an orchestra) to a banquet at the Schönbrunn, the exquisite yellow Habsburg palace outside Vienna.

These were only a few of the royal entertainments; parties and salons went on every day in the great houses and apartments of Viennese society. Few were more charming—or more closely observed by the secret police—than the perpetual open house held by Fanny von Arnstein and her husband, the baron, Nathan.

Fanny von Arnstein, daughter of a rich and distinguished Jewish financier in Berlin, was then in her 50s, tall, slim, and blue-eyed. She was fluent in French, English, and Italian, as well as German; she played the piano and sang delightfully; and she had been hosting a lively salon in her huge apartment for 35 years, since shortly after she arrived as a young bride in 1776. By the turn of the century, everyone—Jews, Gentiles, aristocrats, intellectuals, artists, and businessmen—came to Arnstein's home. "Towards every stranger she is almost equally civil, and knows how to create a pleasant relationship with him immediately," a young Bavarian visitor once observed. "From midday about twelve until well after midnight one here meets the most select company, to whom one has daily access, without special invitation. One comes without great ceremony and goes without taking formal leave; all the tiresome etiquette of the higher circles is banned; the spirit, freed from the restraining fetters of propriety, breathes more freely here."

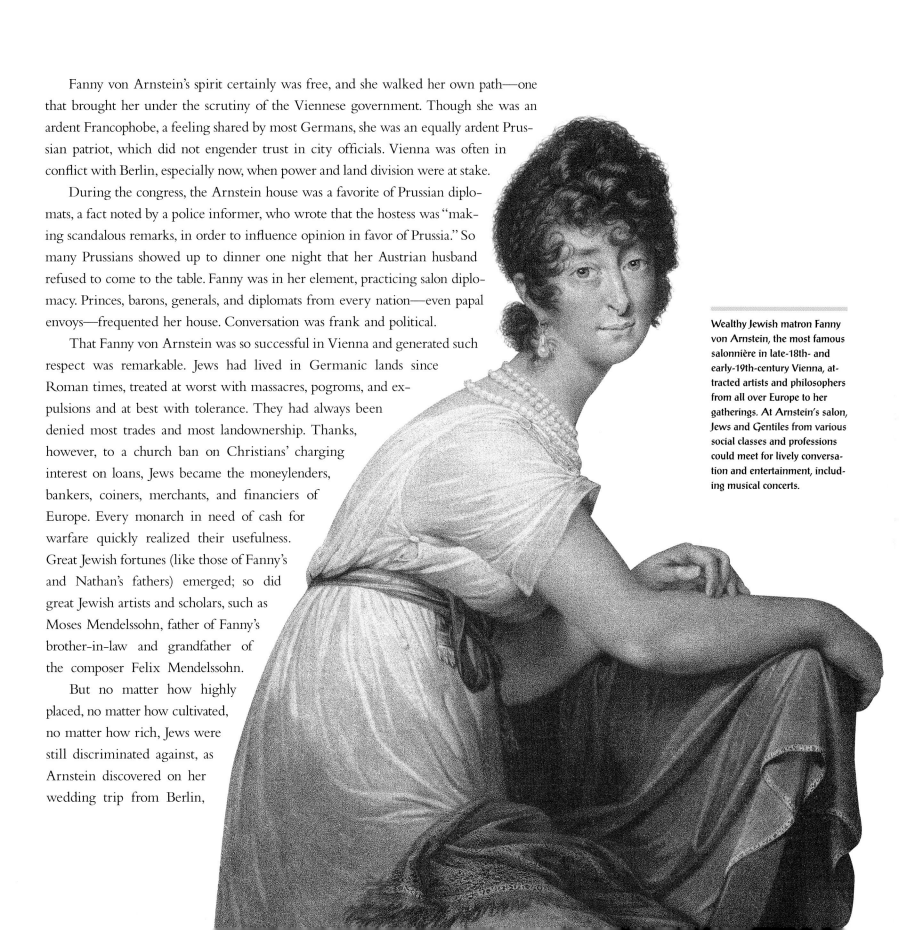

Fanny von Arnstein's spirit certainly was free, and she walked her own path—one that brought her under the scrutiny of the Viennese government. Though she was an ardent Francophobe, a feeling shared by most Germans, she was an equally ardent Prussian patriot, which did not engender trust in city officials. Vienna was often in conflict with Berlin, especially now, when power and land division were at stake.

During the congress, the Arnstein house was a favorite of Prussian diplomats, a fact noted by a police informer, who wrote that the hostess was "making scandalous remarks, in order to influence opinion in favor of Prussia." So many Prussians showed up to dinner one night that her Austrian husband refused to come to the table. Fanny was in her element, practicing salon diplomacy. Princes, barons, generals, and diplomats from every nation—even papal envoys—frequented her house. Conversation was frank and political.

That Fanny von Arnstein was so successful in Vienna and generated such respect was remarkable. Jews had lived in Germanic lands since Roman times, treated at worst with massacres, pogroms, and expulsions and at best with tolerance. They had always been denied most trades and most landownership. Thanks, however, to a church ban on Christians' charging interest on loans, Jews became the moneylenders, bankers, coiners, merchants, and financiers of Europe. Every monarch in need of cash for warfare quickly realized their usefulness. Great Jewish fortunes (like those of Fanny's and Nathan's fathers) emerged; so did great Jewish artists and scholars, such as Moses Mendelssohn, father of Fanny's brother-in-law and grandfather of the composer Felix Mendelssohn.

But no matter how highly placed, no matter how cultivated, no matter how rich, Jews were still discriminated against, as Arnstein discovered on her wedding trip from Berlin,

Wealthy Jewish matron Fanny von Arnstein, the most famous salonnière in late-18th- and early-19th-century Vienna, attracted artists and philosophers from all over Europe to her gatherings. At Arnstein's salon, Jews and Gentiles from various social classes and professions could meet for lively conversation and entertainment, including musical concerts.

when brutal Dresden toll collectors demanded from the young couple a toll applied only to cattle, pigs, and Jews. A special passport purchased by her father-in-law exempted them, but she never forgot the ugly incident. When she arrived in Vienna, she found a city even more anti-Semitic than Berlin, partly due to the virulent prejudice of the then-empress, Maria Theresa.

When Maria Theresa's son, the reformer Joseph II, succeeded to the throne, he issued the Edict of Toleration. This 1781 edict allowed Jews "to learn all manner of handicrafts and trades here and elsewhere from Christian masters" and to practice these as well as painting, sculpture, and the liberal arts. Jews now could set up factories and workshops. They could bear arms for their country and rent (but not own) residences in the city. They no longer had to wear an identifying yellow patch (abolished almost a century before in Berlin). These changes were heralded throughout Europe as the first steps in the emancipation of Jewry. Jews hardly had equal rights, however. They could not conduct public religious services, own a synagogue, or maintain Hebrew presses.

Ironically, though Fanny von Arnstein might hate Napoleon's actions against her homeland, he had enforced in all conquered lands the French edict of 1791 that rescinded all laws against Jews. The edict was withdrawn when he was defeated. Delegations of German Jews were at the Congress of Vienna, asking for their rights back. All they got was a vague statement recommending emancipation. As German nationalism developed in the coming decades, even enlightened tolerance would recede.

Nevertheless, in 1815, the Arnsteins—the first Jewish family ennobled in Vienna, in return for financial services to the Crown—stood at the peak of the second rank of the aristocracy. Fanny von Arnstein's entertainments reached their apogee with a patriotic ball she staged with her husband during the congress. The crowd was too large even for their apartment, so they hired a public ballroom. The affair began with a concert, which was followed by dancing and a lavish supper. The decorations made

spring of winter: The halls were filled with imported rare flowers and entire trees bearing cherries, peaches, and apricots for the guests to pick. It was a triumph for Arnstein, who would live for only another three years, dying from illness in June 1818.

The Arnstein ball was in the style, if perhaps not on the scale, of the entertainments of the nobility. Beethoven's supporter Count Razumovsky outdid himself at the Russian Embassy: One of his suppers included oysters from Brittany and Belgium, pineapples from the czar's Moscow hothouses, and cherries brought from St. Petersburg. Russian dancers entertained after dinner; then everyone did the daring new waltz.

Razumovsky also staged the concert to benefit Beethoven on

GYMNASTICS AND NATIONALISM

Young men climb ropes, ladders, and poles; balance on a wooden beam; swing on pairs of rings; and dangle in various positions as they exercise in the manner prescribed by 19th-century German educator and nationalist Friedrich Ludwig Jahn. Jahn—whom future generations would consider the father of gymnastics—believed such training was morally as well as physically uplifting. In 1811 in the city of Berlin, he opened the first gymnasium, which he also used as a forum for expressing his nationalistic views. Seven years later, authorities imprisoned him for propagating subversive ideas, then barred him from teaching after his release in 1823.

November 29, 1814. Beethoven conducted his Seventh Symphony, but there was more: In a burst of patriotic fervor, he had written a tribute to the Austrian emperor, a cantata in honor of the congress, and the crowd-pleasing *Wellington's Victory*. Complete with thundering drums and cannon salutes, it honored the duke of Wellington's 1812 defeat of French troops in Spain. There was also a polonaise for the czarina, who granted the composer a private audience and a handsome honorarium. Much as he might protest his poverty, Beethoven emerged from the congress well fortified financially and at the peak of his popularity.

Beethoven had other problems, however. By 1816, he had to use an ear trumpet for conversation; two years later, his friends communicated in writing in what he called "conversation books." Other conditions developed as well, including cirrhosis of the liver. His eccentricities increased: He stumbled about the city in a long overcoat, his hair alarmingly long and unkempt, pausing to make entries in his notebook, humming imagined melodies. He railed against censorship and the emperor's "paralytic regime." The police let him alone, because of his eminence—and because he seemed simply mad.

In his soundless solitude, Beethoven continued to compose, the music echoing in his mind. These last years produced not only his late, introspective quartets, but the matchless Ninth Symphony, built around his beloved Schiller's "Ode to Joy" with its glorious affirmation of universal love. The composer himself stood on the podium at its premiere in 1824, turning the pages of his score while others conducted, so deaf he could not hear the thunderous applause.

Three years later the man whom many would consider the greatest composer of all time died. Eight Kapellmeisters carried the coffin as his long funeral procession wound through the streets of Vienna, which were lined with thousands of mourning Viennese.

In 1815, the Congress of Vienna formed the German Confederation, a loose political association that left most power with the state governments. During the decades that followed, members of the confederation found peace from the depredations of foreign armies, from the bewildering shifts of territory and rulers, and from the desperate poverties of war. It proved to be peace at a price, however. Austria, for instance, was still ruled, as it had been since 1792, by Francis I (nephew of Joseph II). He ruled first as the Holy Roman emperor Francis II and later as Francis I, emperor of Austria. He saw himself as the father of his people. During the upheavals of the French Revolution, he had tried to ensure that his people were free from "all dangerous impressions that might have been instilled in any class of subjects by sneaking agitators."

The emperor meant liberal or republican ideas, and he suppressed them with an effective organization of secret police, strengthened after the congress by Austrian prince Klemens Metternich and his infamous Karlsbad Decrees. Issued by the confederation in 1819 to eliminate threats to the authority of the now-restored old regime, the decrees ushered in a time of general censorship

and outlawed groups calling for an end to the confederation and the establishment of a true national government. Liberal clubs and other groups were disbanded; their leaders were jailed or emigrated to America. Trials, held without juries, were conducted in secret. The press was severely censored.

Surveillance was everywhere. All university lectures were

The idealized lifestyle of the Biedermeier era is epitomized in pictures from the 1820s and '30s: At left, a family blissfully starts its day as mother clears away the dishes and father visits with his sons and daughters before sending them off to school. Above, a young woman watches her children at play, which for many included riding to adventure atop a rocking horse *(far left)*. People of the era believed home and family gave life its true meaning.

supervised by government officials to ensure correctness of thought. All travelers—not only foreign travelers and people moving among the various states of the new German Confederation, but even people moving from one town to another in their own states—had to have passports.

Despite the political oppression, this was a period of rising prosperity for many Germans, especially the bourgeoisie. As in the rest of Europe, the bourgeoisie were beginning to assume leadership of society. In contrast to more industrialized nations—for the German lands were still largely agricultural—they were rarely capitalists. (After the depredations of the wars, there was little capital.) But German education, however censored, was among the most thorough in the world, and education was the key to success. The members of the new middle class were professionals—university professors, schoolmasters, journalists, lawyers, doctors. Peace—and carefulness about political activity—allowed them to establish comfortable lives.

The era, which assumed a middle-class intimacy and coziness, would later become known as the Biedermeier. The appellation was originally a joke name used as a pseudonym for the risibly awful verses of an obscure village schoolmaster, published during the 1850s in a humor magazine. First applied ironically, it later came to signify nostalgia for an age that, whatever its undercurrents, seemed comfortable and safe. The Biedermeier was in many respects a reaction against what people perceived as the wild excesses of the Romantics.

The admired house of the period was a comfortable middle-class villa, not a palace, and it was furnished with easy chairs and soft sofas, small curving tables and chairs rather than with the grand Neoclassic pieces of the Napoleonic era. Houses were filled with plants and flowers—this was an age that loved nature, not wild and romantic but well tamed. Children's toys lay about, signs of familial security. The preferred pictures were flower studies and realistic family portraits.

In this romanticized scene, the Grimm brothers sit in a peasant's home surrounded by children and chickens while they interview storyteller Dorothea Viehmann. In reality, Viehmann told her stories to Jacob and Wilhelm over coffee in their comfortable apartment.

People joined literary societies, choral societies, and societies for the advancement of music. They went to concerts at public halls, not royal theaters, and they frequented new public museums. At their informal gatherings, people played instruments and sang to amuse themselves: The composer Franz Schubert's lieder were particularly suited to such occasions. Schubert himself could be found in attendance at the "literary tea table" of the historical novelist Karoline Pichler. Pichler's style of gathering had replaced the extravagant entertainment of Fanny von Arnstein's earlier salons, for even the aristocracy had come under the influence of this new age. The atmosphere at these teas was not the liberal cosmopolitan one of the generation before, but pro-Austrian and pro-emperor.

Schubert was typical of the period. The composer, who lived from 1797 to 1828, worked at the same time as Beethoven but moved in very different circles. He had no noble or royal patrons. He had a wide circle of young, middle-class friends, many, such as the painter Moritz von Schwind and the playwright Franz Grillparzer, destined for later fame. All were disillusioned by what they saw as the hypocrisy of German life, but they were not activists. They met instead in social clubs to discuss literature, produce plays and spoofs, and generally have a good time.

They also met frequently for *Schubertiaden*—parties at their homes or at inns or picnics in the country at which they listened to Schubert's highly individual music, danced to his playing, and enjoyed themselves. Among his thousand or so works were lieder, chamber music, masses for Vienna's churches, symphonies, operas, and incomparable piano music, most of it remaining unpublished and unknown until years after his death (probably from then-incurable syphilis) at age 31. In his few years, this musician of the Biedermeier burned—like another of his contemporaries who died young, British poet John Keats—with a gemlike flame.

six grandchildren on a meager income, had journeyed from the countryside that day to sell vegetables. But the men seated before her had been in the market for folk tales, not onions. Bribed, perhaps, with the offer of hot coffee, she had climbed the stairs to their rooms and begun sharing the stories heard long ago in her youth. The two men listening so intently to her and taking notes were Jacob and Wilhelm Grimm.

The Grimm brothers were in many ways the Biedermeier ideal. Avid students of Germany's past, they were devoted to their work, to their family, and to each other. They lived frugally, seeking only enough money to continue their scholarly pursuits.

Born in 1785 and 1786, respectively, Jacob and Wilhelm were raised in the principality of Hesse-Kassel, the sons of a

"*I am moved and touched, for on all the pages his picture stands before me.*"

The Biedermeier did not reject everything valued by the Romantics. From them, it inherited a deep curiosity about the past—specifically, German history. Philosophers and historians drawn to the idea of unified German states delved into history to show their fellow Germans that they had common, deep, and enduring bonds. Among these scholars was Friedrich Karl von Savigny, whose chief study was legal history: He tried to discover through it the nature of the German *Volk* (the people), to uncover a national identity. His work inspired the efforts of brothers named Jacob and Wilhelm Grimm, who brought the world the magic of fairy tales.

One day in the early 1800s, an impoverished tailor's widow named Dorothea Viehmann sat in an apartment in the town of Kassel spinning tales. Viehmann, who supported a daughter and

prosperous lawyer with a large, happy family. When the brothers were only boys, their father died, and the family descended into near poverty. Nevertheless, they were able to study law at the University of Marburg. "Lack of money is an inducement to diligence and work and inculcates the noble pride which the consciousness of one's own merit maintains with regard to that which others are given by their status and wealth," wrote Jacob, with typical middle-class pride.

But under Savigny's influence, and inspired by their own idealistic hopes for a united Germany, they abandoned law to explore early German language, literature, and folklore. They taught themselves to read Old High German, Gothic, Old Norse, and Old English, among other languages.

This was not accomplished without hardship: Jacob and Wilhelm had to support three younger brothers and a sister, which they did as librarians, first in Hesse and then (ironically enough for two proud German nationalists) in Jérôme Bonaparte's new Kingdom of Westphalia. After 1815, they worked again in the Hessian city of Kassel, then at Göttingen University in the state of Hannover, and later at Berlin University.

The brothers were inseparable. Even when Wilhelm married, Jacob remained a part of the household. And their quiet work together produced monumental results: They wanted, Jacob wrote, "to follow modestly the profound spirit of the language." To that end, in 1819 he produced his *German Grammar,* which ran to four volumes and 4,000 pages and sold out within a year. It documented the evolution of all the Germanic dialects from fourth-century Gothic to the early 19th century and demonstrated how they were related to Greek and Latin in the great Indo-European family of languages. With Wilhelm, he began the vast *German Dictionary,* which set the standard for all dictionaries to come.

The brothers' most famous general work, however, began years before in 1806. Inspired by their study of language and by the Romantic view of folk song, myth, and legend as relics of a golden age, the Grimm brothers started collecting local folk tales, which they believed belonged to all Germans. Their sources were books and people, mostly friends and acquaintances who had heard the tales from nursemaids and governesses. The Wild family, living next-door to the brothers, was a primary source. Rudolf Wild, an apothecary, had several daughters—among them Wilhelm's future wife—who as children had heard many tales from their old nanny.

Another valuable source was an old soldier named Johann Friedrich Krause, who bartered tales in

Tales from the Grimm Brothers

Though the Grimms worked together on their first book of folk tales, Wilhelm edited the subsequent volumes, following the style he and Jacob had established. Wilhelm reworked tales from one edition to the next, altering them to include more of the flavor of oral tradition and to make them more suitable for children. He deleted many of the frankly sexual elements and emphasized the different roles of women and men.

The Grimms' 1812 and 1857 editions present very different Rapunzels. In the earlier one, the king climbed Rapunzel's amazing hair to join her in her prison tower, and "thus they lived merrily and joyfully for a certain time." Rapunzel's jailer suspected nothing until the prisoner complained, "My clothes have become too tight." They were tight because she was pregnant. By 1857, Rapunzel was a more modest maid, whom the king quickly asked to marry him. The couple then planned Rapunzel's escape, rather than retiring to her bedroom.

A revision to Snow White's story offered a chance to list all the duties expected of a good housewife. In the original, the dwarfs tell Snow White she can stay with them if she will cook. Later, they tell her she can remain "if you keep house for us and cook, sew, make the beds, wash and knit, and keep everything tidy and clean.... In the evening, when we come home, dinner must be ready."

Modern storytellers, too, have revised the tales. Newer versions of Cinderella vary greatly from the Grimms' story, which is synopsized below:

A dying woman told her daughter to be "good and pious" and promised to watch over her from heaven. The girl obeyed, but her life darkened

A stricken Snow White lies in her glass coffin, guarded by one of the seven dwarfs. The Grimm brothers heard the story of Snow White from Marie Müller, the nanny for a neighbor's children.

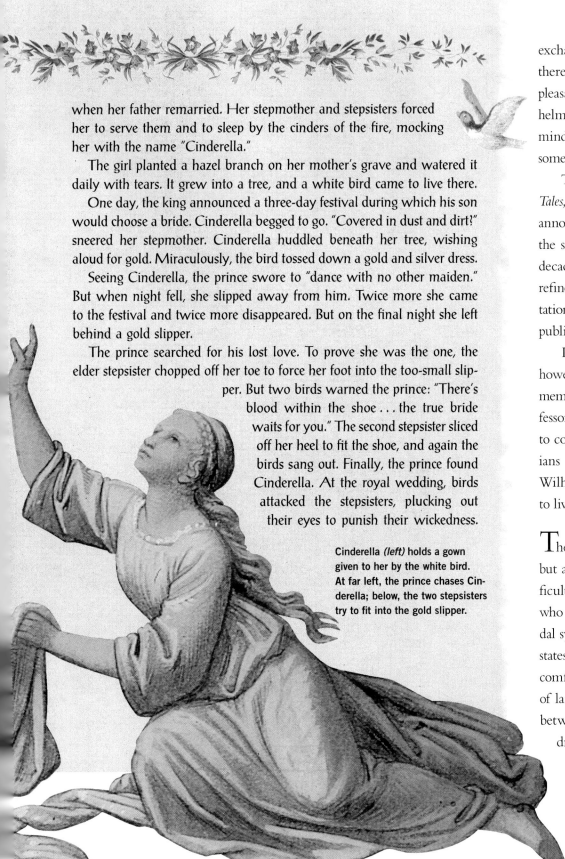

when her father remarried. Her stepmother and stepsisters forced her to serve them and to sleep by the cinders of the fire, mocking her with the name "Cinderella."

The girl planted a hazel branch on her mother's grave and watered it daily with tears. It grew into a tree, and a white bird came to live there.

One day, the king announced a three-day festival during which his son would choose a bride. Cinderella begged to go. "Covered in dust and dirt!" sneered her stepmother. Cinderella huddled beneath her tree, wishing aloud for gold. Miraculously, the bird tossed down a gold and silver dress.

Seeing Cinderella, the prince swore to "dance with no other maiden." But when night fell, she slipped away from him. Twice more she came to the festival and twice more disappeared. But on the final night she left behind a gold slipper.

The prince searched for his lost love. To prove she was the one, the elder stepsister chopped off her toe to force her foot into the too-small slipper. But two birds warned the prince: "There's blood within the shoe ... the true bride waits for you." The second stepsister sliced off her heel to fit the shoe, and again the birds sang out. Finally, the prince found Cinderella. At the royal wedding, birds attacked the stepsisters, plucking out their eyes to punish their wickedness.

Cinderella *(left)* holds a gown given to her by the white bird. At far left, the prince chases Cinderella; below, the two stepsisters try to fit into the gold slipper.

exchange for the Grimms' discarded trousers. Then there was Dorothea Viehmann. "She has a strong, pleasant face, and a clear sharp look in her eyes," Wilhelm wrote. "She retains these old tales firmly in her mind, a gift, as she says, not possessed by everyone, as some cannot keep anything in their heads at all."

The first edition of *The Children's and Household Tales,* published in 1812 with 86 stories and scholarly annotations, sold slowly, but that would change as the stories gained in popularity. Over the following decades, the brothers would publish additional tales, refine stories in subsequent editions, drop the annotations, and publish smaller collections to interest the public in the large volumes.

It was the brothers' work in the field of language, however, that brought them honorary doctorates, memberships in learned societies, and offers of professorships. Despite such accolades, they were content to continue in their undemanding positions as librarians in Kassel, pursuing their research and writing. Wilhelm wrote in 1825, "My wish is only to be able to live in simple and natural circumstances as before."

The Grimms did well from humble beginnings, but as the century progressed, life became more difficult for Germans in general, particularly for those who lived on the land. In the 19th century, the feudal system was being dismantled in Prussia and other states. Though this left some former serfs with small, comfortable farms, many more became a huge class of landless laborers. Some two million left the land between 1820 and 1860, emigrating to America or drifting into the small, walled cities and towns, which had no room for them. The poor lived in

Clad in festive Bavarian costumes, a couple performs a church dedication dance. Resurrecting such dances was part of a movement of people seeking to unite the German states by embracing the traditions of the past. German nationalism would gain momentum after the 1848 revolution.

damp, and sometimes flooded, cellars or in places like Berlin's Voigtland district, where 2,500 people were housed in 400 rooms.

The difficult economic situation began to affect almost everyone, not just peasants and workers. Middle-class civil servants and shopkeepers alike could barely make ends meet. Things were at their worst in the 1840s, when failures of the grain and potato harvests caused famines and great hardship.

Yet it was not just poverty or the fear of slipping into it that was embittering people. Among all classes, the constant censorship imposed by the German governments, the harassment by officials, the imprisonment of dissidents, all fed an almost silent rage at police-state tactics.

People fought back, hoping to alter the system of government through local uprisings and protests. Even the scholarly Grimm brothers protested in their own way. In 1837, Jacob, Wilhelm, and five colleagues at the University of Göttingen were expelled from their posts—and the state—for refusing to forswear allegiance to a constitution that Hannover's new king had revoked. They eventually found a home in Berlin at the invitation of King Frederick William IV, a supporter of the humanities who was thought to have liberal sympathies.

The general atmosphere of the times was complicated by a kind of despairing fatalism among the ruling classes. Revolution must come, they seemed to feel. "I am an old physician and can distinguish between temporary and fatal diseases," that wily Austrian autocrat Prince Klemens Metternich told a friend in 1847, "and we now face one of the latter."

Perhaps it was this fatalism that made the remarkable capitulations of 1848 inevitable. Within weeks of the revolt in Paris, peasant riots occurred in those German states that had not yet abolished serfdom—Nassau, Baden, and Württemberg. Castles were put to the torch and estate records destroyed. Huge crowds surrounded the palace in Karlsruhe, capital of Baden, demanding a constitution and a free press.

During the spring months, Hungary, Austria's Italian states, and Austria's satellites in Bohemia and the east all rose in revolt against rule from Vienna. In Vienna itself, rioting students and workers took control of the streets, demanding an end to troop occupation, institution of a civic guard, abolition of censorship, and a constitution.

In Berlin on March 18, massive rioting broke out between the military and groups of students, artisans, teachers, and homeowners. The civilians set up barricades in the streets; the troops cut them down whenever they could reach them. It was a dreadful night, wrote Wilhelm Grimm, whose students had escorted him safely home through the gunfire. "For a good fourteen hours, from two to three thousand people battled the troops violently in the streets. The rattling volleys of rifle fire, the roar of the cannon and the shells were frightful." By the morning of the 19th, most of the city was under military control.

At that point, the king, Frederick William, issued a proclamation to his "true and dear Berliners," promising that the troops would be withdrawn as soon as the barricades came down. The city calmed. A civic guard was enrolled to maintain peace. Frederick William made another populist gesture. He announced that a Prussian assembly would convene to discuss uniting with the rest of Germany and then rode in procession through his capital, accompanied by various princes and generals, all of them wrapped not in the colors of Prussia but in the black, red, and gold of the German Confederation.

The reasons behind the king's behavior involved, no doubt, his idea of a united Germany with himself at the head. It was no wonder that he had been thinking about it. Even as the various German states abolished serfdom, appointed liberal ministries, and granted various personal freedoms, the idea came to the fore of uniting the states and principalities that made up the German Confederation. At the end of March, a "pre-Parliament" of 500 to 600 liberal, democratic, and republican delegates from the past and present legislatures of the various states began gathering in Frankfurt. Among the representatives who would attend the meeting was Jacob Grimm, described in the press as "every inch a German." No one had forgotten his stand at Göttingen. As one editorial commented, both Jacob and Wilhelm "sacrificed their livelihood for noble principles. The brothers Grimm deserve the respect of all Germans."

Jacob himself announced, "I am for a free, united fatherland under the rule of a powerful king and against all republican longings." Delegates listened to him with courtesy and respect despite his tendency to wander a bit in long-winded speeches at the meetings. In both political position and verbosity, he was like most representatives at the Parliament. The majority were liberals who wanted to create a monarchical federal state (in opposition to a small group of radicals who wanted a republic, and to socialists), and they talked at great length about it, all through the summer and autumn.

Most of the delegates were frightened by socialist agitation— as indeed were most of the German middle class. As one member put it, "We are dealing here only with civic equality, not with that crude, materialistic, communistic equality which seeks to do away with all natural differences."

The Parliament finally proposed a German constitution that united the German states, removing much of their individual authority. On the question of Austria, with its many non-German peoples, they suggested dividing the German-speaking from the non-German-speaking lands. Austria—whose armies by now had destroyed most of the insurrections against the empire and which was busily working with a new, pragmatic legislature—refused any concessions, and from then on the Parliament thought in terms of a Germany united under Prussia.

Events in Prussia had been moving quickly, however. In October, Frederick William, backed by fervently royalist troops, had declared his throne in danger and dissolved the Revolutionary assembly. He then granted to Prussia a limited constitution, reserving for himself the power of absolute veto. When the Frankfurt Parliamentary Assembly offered him the crown of a united Germany, Frederick declined. Refusing to accept a title that came from the assembly and not from the German princes, he called it "a crown from the gutter," adding that it would be "a dog collar fastened round my neck by the sovereign German people."

The failure of the revolution in Prussia doomed the pan-German Parliament—which, after all, had no real power of its own. Various factors, including their own internal divisions and the fear they inspired in the German middle class, doomed the radical elements in politics. In fact, though some smaller states retained their constitutions, most other states repealed the political reforms. The old German Confederation was reinstated under Austrian leadership. Disappointed by the failure of the revolution, Jacob Grimm retired from this brief political foray to continue the Grimms' work on language and history.

A new edition of the Grimms' fairy tales appeared in 1858; Wilhelm died the following year. Jacob lived another four years, never quite recovering from his brother's death.

By illuminating ancient German culture through the common elements in its language and folk tales, the brothers helped shape a new sense of German identity. The failure of the 1848 revolutions and the brothers' deaths coincided with the passing of an age of great fervor and creativity. After Wilhelm's death, Jacob delivered a memorial address about his brother. When reading Wilhelm's work, he said, "I am moved and touched, for on all the pages his picture stands before me and I recognize his distinctive path." The same could be said for Jacob, as well, and for all the other creative spirits who flourished during the first half of Germany's 19th century.

Romantic Painting

Painting, wrote critic Friedrich von Schlegel in 1803, should capture "the incomprehensible union of soul, expression and individuality." European painters of the late 18th and early 19th centuries strove to obtain that union in remarkably diverse ways, making Romanticism less a distinct style than an attitude marked by rebellion against the stifling norms of Classical formalism. The

Enlightenment had sought to tame nature with reason; now Romantic artists set out to penetrate nature's soul through solitary contemplation. "Follow without hesitation the voice of your inner self," declared German painter Caspar David Friedrich, whose *Wanderer above the Mists (above)* embodied the individualistic, tumultuous spirit of the new age.

A Fresh Perspective

In the traditional hierarchy of artistic genres, landscape painting languished below historical painting, which edified the viewer through ennobling emblems and events. By championing the notion of an individual's communion with nature, however, young artists brought newfound respect to landscape and established it as the preeminent Romantic subject. They ridiculed imitation—British "gentlemen in their wigs and jockey caps," galloping through the Italian countryside, sniffed one of the new practitioners, Englishman John Constable. In search of fresh, original scenes, Romantic landscape artists stopped imitating paintings and turned to studying nature itself.

They excelled at capturing its fleeting states. Constable's intimate views of his native Suffolk were achieved after closely observing that region's interplay of sky, wind, and sun. Rejecting the brown tones of Old Master landscapes, he infused his canvases with a brilliant natural white that dapples rustling leaves and reflects off rippling water, producing a scintillating effect of nature in flux.

Constable's contemporary, English painter Joseph Mallord William Turner, started from the same premise—a close study of nature—and produced landscapes that were utterly different. "Airy visions, painted with tinted steam," Constable complained of Turner's paintings, which were so subjective and supercharged with color and light that the original scene was nearly obliterated. Posterity would disagree with Constable: Turner's talent for conveying the immensity of landscape and the transitory effects of atmosphere make him one of the greatest landscapists of any age.

The sky, remarked Constable, is "the key note and the chief organ of sentiment." His genius for expressing its changeable qualities makes scenes like this one–*Dedham Lock and Mill* (1820) *(left)*–distinctly Romantic.

If John Constable was a naturalist, William Turner was a painter of landscapes best described as visionary. In *Norham Castle, Sunrise* (c. 1835-1840) *(right)*, Turner's subject is obscured by light and mood.

Lure of the Exotic

The Romantics cultivated passionate interest in exotic people, places, and cultures, both past and present. Ancient civilizations and foreigners were seen as primitive and thus more attuned to the natural world than were contemporary Europeans imprisoned in the artifices of conventional society. Artists sought out ancient ruins such as Stonehenge, pictured in the scene below by Constable. Some, like Frenchman Eugène Delacroix, ventured farther afield to collect impressions of different lands. As might be expected from a movement that celebrated the artist's individual genius, works portraying this quest for the exotic were diverse in style and subject. Yet they all bear the Romantic exaltation of the sensuous, emotional, or mysterious.

In 1832 Delacroix was thrilled by "primitives" in North Africa. "I have Greeks and Romans on my doorstep," he exulted from Tangier. "I now know what they were really like." His African memories and sketches fueled his imagination for the next 30 years and, by enhancing his sensuous use of color and light, ultimately helped shape art's Impressionist movement.

Eugène Delacroix gained entrance to a harem in North Africa and later re-created the scene in *Women of Algiers* (1834) *(right)*. Its languorous sensuousness—the somnolent eyes, colorful fabrics, and luminous play of light and shadow—prompted Impressionist Pierre-Auguste Renoir to swear he could smell the incense.

In *Stonehenge* (1836) *(left)*, the monumental slabs and the evanescent panorama of clouds and rainbow are united by what Constable called "the light of nature, the mother of all that is valuable where an appeal to the soul is required." Romantics saw the ruins as a testament to the grandeur and futility of human endeavor.

One of the most notorious and plagiarized works of the Romantic era was John Henry Fuseli's *Nightmare* (1791). The erotic, marblelike figure of the sleeping woman contrasts with the startling vision of the stallion, with bulging, voyeuristic eyes and ghostly mane, which has its head thrust through the curtains.

Envisioning the Sublime

In their rebellion against accepted strictures of "good taste," Romantic artists wholeheartedly embraced the cult of the sublime. The sublime, wrote Edmund Burke, is anything that stirs "the strongest emotion which the mind is capable of feeling"— terror, pain, pleasure, and above all, awe before the unknown. Two subjects filled with such emotions held great appeal for aspiring artists: dreams and visions.

Swiss-born John Henry Fuseli, who worked in London, exercised enormous influence in this area of Romantic art. His paintings mined the psyche's dark recesses, exploring deviant eroticism and dementia to make "visible," in the words of one reviewer, "the vague and insubstantial phantoms which haunt the oppressed imagination." Known to his contemporaries as "Principal Hobgoblin Painter to the Devil," Fuseli was said to eat a plateful of raw pork chops before going to bed in order to induce more vivid dreams for use in his art.

Fuseli befriended English poet-painter William Blake, a visionary recluse adamantly opposed to the teachings of the British Royal Academy. Blake illustrated his own mystical poems as well as scenes from the Bible and other literary works with hand-tinted engravings and watercolors. Beset by nocturnal visions of angels since childhood, he developed the habit of waiting for his visitors with pencil and paper ready; as soon as a vision would appear, he feverishly set to work recording it. A story circulated about Blake's once having been shut up in a lunatic asylum. But that did not detract from his reputation: The Romantics, who felt that genius verged on madness, had a profound respect for artistic eccentrics.

Although he was deeply influenced by Classical art and literature, William Blake illustrated Dante's *Inferno* in his own passionate, visionary style. In *Circle of the Lustful* (1824-1827), Dante watches as a whirlwind sweeps away doomed lovers who have given up their lives to passion.

The Power of Nature

Nowhere was the Romantic attraction to the sublime better manifested than in majestic scenes of nature that inspired awe and terror—avalanches, precipitous cliffs, cascading waterfalls, towering mountain peaks, and as in the two paintings here, the churning sea. Poet William Wordsworth wrote that nature's soaring prospects and violent unpredictability had "ample power to chasten and subdue" the witness. Humankind, according to a common Romantic notion, was no match for the elements.

This was one of the enduring themes of William Turner's art. His keen sense of the wild and savage aspects of nature's sublime power was not just intuitive: The painting of a snowstorm at sea *(right)* was the result of an obsessive personal experience. Turner happened to be aboard the steamboat *Ariel*

off Harwich, England, when a storm whipped up. Persuading the crew to lash him to a spar on deck, he remained there for four long hours while the sirens of wind and snow and seawater lashed his skin. Some uncomprehending critics called the painting that grew out of this experience "a mass of soapsuds and whitewash." "Soapsuds and whitewash!" Turner chafed. "I wonder what they think the sea's like?"

Caspar David Friedrich's scene below is radically different— it is painted in the style of a meticulous draftsman—yet nonetheless makes a similar point. The huge, almost photographic slabs of ice in the foreground and the small capsized ship farther away are a haunting Romantic statement about human impotence in the face of nature's brute force.

Friedrich's *Sea of Ice* (1824) *(left)* was inspired by a heart-stopping episode in William Parry's arctic expedition of 1819-1820. With stark realism, the artist—who had studied ice floes on the Elbe River—depicts the huge slabs as they are closing slowly but inexorably around the ship.

The terrifying power of the sea electrifies Turner's *Snowstorm: Steamboat off a Harbour's Mouth* (1842) *(right).* The only suggestion of human presence is the slender mast of the boat, center, which is being engulfed by the raging elements.

CHAPTER THREE

Souls of the Poets

Percy Bysshe Shelley sits among the ruins of the Baths of Caracalla in Rome, where he penned the lyrical drama *Prometheus Unbound* in 1819. The French Revolution inspired English writers such as William Wordsworth, Samuel Taylor Coleridge, and Lord Byron, as well as Shelley, who wrote, "The literature of England has arisen as it were from a new birth."

During the summer of 1797, the air in the west England county of Somerset was filled with rumors. Some peculiar people had moved into Alfoxden House, a spacious nine-bedroom mansion in the village of Holford. The woman, a nervous and high-strung sort of about 25, was as dark as a Gypsy, with gray eyes that glinted with an almost wild light. She went about in all weather, alone or with her brother and a frequent male visitor, and was given to lying down on the grass or heather—unseemly behavior for a woman of her class. Her brother was just a year or two her senior but had the stern, worried look of someone much older. He tramped about in a sturdy brown cotton jacket and striped pantaloons that were out of fashion even for this rural village.

They and their visitor spent most of their time, day and night, walking in the Quantock Hills. They made copious notes and asked suspicious questions about the course of the brook and the river; one even had a spyglass. The local residents were certain that the newcomers were French agents!

Word of these suspicions reached government officials, who promptly dispatched agent James Walsh to investigate. England and

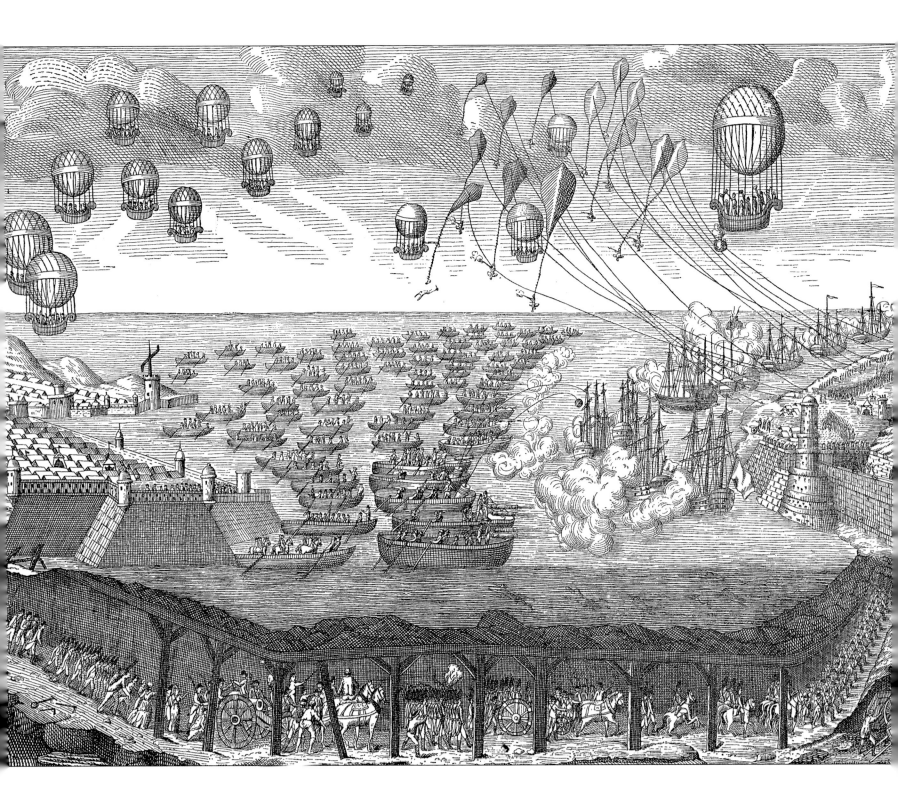

France had been at war for four years, and six months earlier, 1,200 French troops had landed in Wales, just outside the Bristol Channel. Although the invasion had foundered after two days, it had caused panic, and the British feared the French might try again.

After some surreptitious monitoring, Walsh reported that the people in question were only "a mischiefous gang of disaffected Englishmen." At the core of this supposed gang were the poet William Wordsworth, his sister Dorothy, and their friend, poet Samuel Taylor Coleridge, who lived in nearby Nether Stowey.

In the end, Walsh could find nothing incriminating about the trio. Still, in September, the owner of Alfoxden House declared the lease would not be renewed when it expired the following July. The Wordsworths and Coleridge did not let that affect the idyllic months ahead. In fact, their stay at Alfoxden House would come to be called an *annus mirabilis,* or year of wonders. And among the wonders born that year was English Romantic poetry.

The poets' brush with the British government illustrated the strong link—both real and perceived—between English Romanticism and the French Revolution. The initial liberating effect of the Revolution on writers and artists in Europe was undeniable. In the first heady years after 1789, British writers such as Wordsworth and Coleridge thrilled to the promise of a more just and open society. The idea—and ideal—of liberty exerted its effect on British writers such as William Godwin *(Enquiry Concerning Political Justice),* Thomas Paine *(The Rights of Man),* and Mary Wollstonecraft *(Vindication of the Rights of Woman),* who in turn influenced Wordsworth and Coleridge and the next generation of Romantic writers, which included Percy Bysshe Shelley and George Gordon, Lord Byron.

However, when the guillotine became the favored Jacobin instrument of political and social change,

By balloon, ship, and tunnel, Napoleon's army invades England in a fantastic French engraving from 1803. The threat of a real invasion prompted Wordsworth to join a volunteer militia group and compose a series of patriotic poems. Admiral Horatio Nelson's 1805 victory over France at the Battle of Trafalgar quieted English fears.

British writers who had supported the French revolt were bitterly disillusioned. Once England and France went to war in 1793, many outspoken writers retreated as the state began censoring, arresting, and exiling those who voiced radically dissenting views.

Although ceasing to be politically active, British Romantics continued to champion individualism in their work. For the Romantics, social, personal, and artistic liberty meant rejecting objectivity and rationalism in favor of sentiment and instinct. It meant giving free rein to imagination and passion and achieving a oneness with nature that would lead to a more equitable world order. Determined to write and to live according to their beliefs, Byron and Shelley were rebels, outsiders who consciously defied conventional mores. Both came to embody the idea of the Romantic hero and earn a place in Romantic myth by dying young.

Wordsworth's journey to Romanticism began seven years before the annus mirabilis, when he was a student at Cambridge. Swept up by news of the Revolution, in the summer of 1790 he surreptitiously withdrew money set aside for college expenses and with a friend, Robert Jones, left for a 90-day walking tour on the Continent. In France on July 14, the first anniversary of the fall of the Bastille, the young foreigners found themselves surrounded by people seemingly mad with joy. For the next two weeks, as they passed through France en route to the Alps and Italy, Wordsworth and Jones saw people in every town celebrating. Boarding a boat for Lyon, they were transformed from mere observers of the fete to welcome guests. As the poet later described it:

> The supper done,
> With flowing cups elate and happy thoughts
> We rose at signal given, and formed a ring,
> And hand in hand danced round and round the board;
> All hearts were open, every tongue was loud
> With amity and glee . . .

Although he had been sympathetic to the republican movement before landing in France, Wordsworth returned home with a stronger attachment at least partly due to his exhilaration at being a 20-year-old abroad who was warmly received by strangers.

After returning to England, Wordsworth passed his final university exams and spent much of the next year visiting friends and family. He drafted a number of the poems that would become *Descriptive Sketches* (published three years later, in 1793). In them he began to sound the themes to which he would return repeatedly: communion with the spiritual presence in nature, concern for the poor and oppressed, and hope for political change.

But the older members of Wordsworth's family expected more than poetry from him: They expected him to earn a living. His share of his late father's estate would have supported him, but for many years to come that estate would be tied up in litigation over money owed by his father's former employer, James Lowther.

Two of William's uncles (who had been named guardians for him, his three brothers, and his sister after their father died in 1783) suggested a few possibilities: He could immediately accept a position as curate of a parish, or he could continue his education by studying Oriental languages (meaning Hebrew, Aramaic, Latin, and Greek) to become a more learned clergyman or a university tutor. Having little desire to do either, Wordsworth came up with a compromise plan: He would go to France for a year to improve his French; thus equipped, he could become a tutor for young gentlemen making the grand tour. If no tutoring job materialized, he would return to England to be employed.

Wordsworth's uncles agreed, so in late November 1791 he sailed again for the Continent. Knowing that Paris would be too expensive, Wordsworth went to stay in Orléans. There his life took an unexpected turn. He met and fell in love with Annette Vallon. Four years older than the 21-year-old Wordsworth, she was attractive, energetic, and intense. She was also a royalist—and a determined underground fighter against the Revolution.

Wordsworth found himself torn between his republican ideals and his new love. His inner conflict was in many ways a reflection of the turmoil he could see all around him:

> The land all swarmed with passion, like a plain
> Devoured by locusts—Carra, Gorsas—add
> A hundred other names, forgotten now,
> Nor to be heard of more; yet they were powers,
> Like earthquakes, shocks repeated day by day,
> And felt through every nook of town or field.

By the following spring, there were more pressing matters than politics: Vallon was pregnant. Suddenly Wordsworth had to have the means to marry and provide for a family. Without revealing why, his letters home now expressed his growing resolve to become a clergyman.

By the end of December 1792, he had returned to London to arrange his affairs. But before he could do so, France and England went to war. He was unable to go back for Vallon and their daughter, Caroline, while it raged. The war dragged on, and it would be a full decade before the lovers met again. This involuntary desertion would prove a source of much anguish for Wordsworth, a personal torment that would infuse his poetry with images of abandoned mothers and children.

Upon learning that their nephew had a French mistress and an illegitimate child, Wordsworth's uncles withdrew their offer of a future in the church. The poet spent the next four years in a genteel poverty shared with his devoted sister while they waited to come into their inheritance. William's intelligence and compelling personality attracted people, who often provided the brother and sister with housing. In the two years before he and Dorothy moved to Alfoxden House, they lived for free, courtesy of two brothers named Pinney, at Racedown Lodge in Dorset.

Visitors on a grand tour admire the monument of Philopappos in Greece. While expensive, such tours of Europe were often thought preferable to the debauchery of university life. Wealthy guardians would send their charges off under the guidance of a tutor, a position Wordsworth once sought.

They earned a bit of money caring for the small son of a recently widowed friend, Basil Montagu, but it came in irregular installments and barely covered expenses. They had to grow their own food and lived largely on cabbage. It did not help that the winter they spent at Alfoxden was bitterly cold, nor that the average cost of living had doubled because of the war.

Given his own precarious situation, Wordsworth could appreciate what the war was doing to his neighbors in the West Country, especially the poor: "many rich / Sunk down as in a dream among the poor, / And of the poor did many cease to be, / And their place knew them not." Beggars—soldiers returned from the war or women whose husbands had failed to return—became a familiar sight.

Southwestern England was a relatively poor area and would remain so well into the 1800s. As in the rest of England, most people were farm laborers. During the past few decades, many farmers who had worked their village's common land had lost access when these fields were enclosed by wealthier landowners. Once-independent tillers of the soil became tenant farmers or paid workers who found it increasingly difficult to feed their families. To obtain employment, farm hands and other wage laborers attended so-called mop fairs, usually held in late September. At the fairs, workers stood in the streets wearing tokens indicating their trades. Wagoners, for instance, might have a piece of whipcord tied around their hats, while thatchers might sport a patch of woven straw.

Those working the land toiled year round, dawn to dusk. In the fall or early winter, they plowed the land and then harrowed it—leveling the field, breaking up clods, and removing weeds. During the winter, the wheat, barley, and oats—all called "corn"—harvested during the preceding year were threshed and winnowed. Steam-powered machines would not come into common use for many decades, so each part of the process was powered solely by human or animal muscle.

Through the winter, English farmers also tended their sheep and cattle. Lambs were born in winter, and shepherds watched the flocks night and day to be certain the newborns received enough milk from their mothers.

Corn was sown in the spring, and the sheep were driven out in the mornings to graze in the grass meadows. The animals were brought back to be penned in the cornfields at night to provide fertilizer. In late May, sheep were sheared and driven away from the fields to allow hay to grow for winter fodder. The reaping of hay occurred in June, creating weeks of backbreaking labor, with men swinging the scythes

Amid England's rolling hills and pastureland, walkers pause to admire the view. Like these three, William and Dorothy Wordsworth and Samuel Taylor Coleridge enjoyed exploring the countryside on foot; the invigorating expeditions never failed to inspire the poets. They also enjoyed taking walking tours in other countries; such tours were a popular pastime during the age of English Romanticism.

and women and children gathering and binding the cut hay. Corn was harvested in late summer or early fall. At harvest's end, the landowner threw a feast, called the harvest home. This was also the time when sheep and cattle were sold at market.

The living conditions of the laborers were spartan. Many lived in one-room thatch- or slate-roofed cottages, though people better off might also have a separate kitchen and bedroom. Floors were often beaten earth strewn with straw. Windows were small and glassless, protected only by shutters.

Wordsworth began to hone his ability to empathize not only with poor people but also with those who were old and sick, whether in body or in mind, and to write about them: "the genius of the poet hence / May boldly take his way among mankind / Wherever Nature leads."

Although the Wordsworths' finances were only marginally better when they moved to Somerset in 1797, having Coleridge as a neighbor made all the difference. During July

and August, the poets roamed the countryside, feeling their souls open to the wide sky. The trio began characterizing much of what they saw and experienced as "romantic," meaning somehow strange or strangely beautiful.

Not far from the house was a spot William Wordsworth would remember even 45 years later. He described it vividly: "The brook fell down a sloping rock so as to make a waterfall considerable for that country, and across the pool had fallen a tree, an ash, if I rightly remember, from which rose perpendicularly boughs in search of the light intercepted by the deep shade above. The boughs bore leaves of green that for want of sunshine had faded into almost lily-white; and from the underside of this natural sylvan bridge depended long and beautiful tresses of ivy which waved gently in the breeze that might poetically speaking be called the breath of the waterfall."

In March 1798, Coleridge and the Wordsworths determined that they would go to Germany when the Alfoxden lease expired. Coleridge had recently been granted an annuity of £150 by some wealthy benefactors, but the Wordsworths were woefully short of funds. The poets decided to finance the trip by jointly publishing some poems.

While Coleridge had written "The Rime of the Ancient Mariner," Wordsworth had finished "The Ruined Cottage," a long narrative in blank verse that articulated his belief in the spiritual transcendence inherent in all of nature:

> He was a chosen son:
> To him was given an ear which deeply felt
>   The voice of Nature in the obscure wind,
>   The sounding mountain and the running stream.
>   To every natural form, rock, fruit, and flower,
>   Even the loose stones that cover the highway,
>   He gave a moral life; he saw them feel
>   Or linked them to some feeling.

But instead of building a volume on "Ancient Mariner," "The Ruined Cottage," and similar poems, Wordsworth suddenly decided to make a complete break with his previous work. He began to churn out short poems—ballads and lyrics of a genre familiar to readers of magazine verse of the day. In contrast to the accepted styles, however, these poems spoke with a highly personal voice, were written in conversational language, and concerned ordinary people and the poet's emotional responses to them. "The earliest poets of all nations generally wrote from passion excited by real events," Wordsworth declared. "They wrote naturally."

Over the course of about 10 weeks, from the first week of March to mid-May, Wordsworth produced nearly 1,500 lines of poetry, about a dozen poems. These, plus another seven poems by him and five by Coleridge, including the "Ancient Mariner," would fill a book they entitled *Lyrical Ballads* and published in October 1798. Marking the dawn of a new age, *Lyrical Ballads* was Wordsworth's debut as a Romantic poet.

Four years later, the brief Peace of Amiens allowed Wordsworth to cross to Calais, where he and Dorothy spent August visiting Annette Vallon and nine-year-old Caroline. It was to be the poet's farewell to the love of his youth. Within a few weeks of returning to England, William married Mary Hutchinson, Dorothy's dearest friend. That same year, the Lowther suit was concluded. With his inheritance, William could repay old debts and establish a comfortable place for himself, Mary, and Dorothy at Grasmere, in northwestern England's Lake District.

During the next few years he produced some of his best work, but as his life grew increasingly conventional, so did his writing. The daring author of *Lyrical Ballads* would be submerged in the respectable writer who would serve as poet laureate for the last seven years of his life, until his death in 1850.

In October 1810, Wordsworth's collaborator during the annus mirabilis, Samuel Taylor Coleridge, was in London as a guest of Basil Montagu, who hoped to help the writer turn his life around. Wordsworth, with whom Coleridge had been living, had privately urged Montagu to reconsider his plans, explaining that Coleridge's opium and alcohol consumption made him unstable. But Montagu had paid no heed.

On October 27, a friend of Coleridge's came by, hoping to indulge in a night of drinking. Montagu limited the amount of wine served, angering the writer. After the guest left, Coleridge confronted his host. Montagu defended his actions by claiming, "Wordsworth has commissioned me to tell you that he has no hope of you, that you have been a rotten drunkard and rotted out your entrails by intemperance, and have been an absolute nuisance in his family."

Coleridge exclaimed, "O this is cruel! This is *base!*"

He fled the house and checked into a hotel. Still distraught, he made his way to the home of his friends Charles and Mary Lamb. When Mary questioned him, he broke into uncontrollable weeping. "Wordsworth has given me up. *He* has no hope of me."

People shop and socialize at the St. James Fair in Bristol. Countryfolk depended on weekly markets and annual fairs to buy and sell food, livestock, clothing, and house and farm implements. Business was conducted in the morning, leaving the afternoon for conversation, games, and dancing.

When told of the incident, Wordsworth denied asking Montagu to tell Coleridge how he felt. But he did not deny the sentiments. In a letter written two years before, Wordsworth had said of Coleridge, "Neither his talents nor his genius mighty as they are, nor his vast information will avail him anything; they are all frustrated by a derangement in his intellectual and moral constitution."

That certainly had not been William or Dorothy Wordsworth's evaluation of the man in 1797. Dorothy wrote to a friend after first meeting Coleridge: "His conversation teems with soul, mind and spirit. . . . His eye . . . speaks every emotion of his animated mind; it has more of the 'poet's eye in a fine frenzy rolling' than I ever witnessed."

Coleridge's creativity during the annus mirabilis seemed to bear out this impression. He produced not only the "Ancient Mariner" but "Kubla Khan" as well, an exotic poem with almost mystical origins. According to Coleridge, he was out walking when a sudden bout of dysentery forced him to take refuge at a farmhouse. As a self-prescribed treatment, he consumed opium. During the state of reverie that followed, the lines of "Kubla Khan" came to him. Emerging from this state, he immediately started writing:

In Xanadu did Kubla Khan
A stately pleasure-dome decree:
Where Alph, the sacred river, ran
Through caverns measureless to man
Down to a sunless sea.

He penned a few more verses before a visitor interrupted him. By the time he returned to his task, the poet claimed, he had forgotten the rest of the poem and never finished it.

Coleridge's story of the origins of "Kubla Khan" contained the essential elements that would shape his life: great talent and imagination crippled by a lack of resolve and the use of opium. By 1800, Coleridge was consuming large doses of the drug, and his health was deteriorating. He suffered from horrible, sweat-drenched nightmares and complained of joint swelling, nausea, rheumatism, dizziness, and diarrhea and constipation. All were conditions experienced by opium addicts and were caused by withdrawal from the drug, a fact not widely known until the mid 1820s. Many

"A noticeable Man with large grey eyes," an observer said of Samuel Taylor Coleridge, shown here in 1795 at age 23. Two years later, Coleridge, inspired by his association with Wordsworth, soared to new poetic heights. But by 1801 he had plunged into drug addiction and despair, proclaiming, "The poet is dead in me."

William Wordsworth sat for this portrait in 1798, the year that he and Coleridge published their book of poetry, *Lyrical Ballads*. Coleridge was in awe of his collaborator, saying, "I speak with heart-felt sincerity ... when I tell you, that I feel myself *a little man by his* side."

patients undergoing withdrawal symptoms thought their illnesses were recurring and resumed taking the drug.

Though Coleridge grew ashamed of his addiction, during the early 19th century opium was considered a legitimate treatment for many ailments, including alcoholism, cholera, gout, hay fever, insomnia, and tuberculosis. It was also used liberally as a tranquilizer. Working-class women gave opium elixirs such as Mother Bailey's Quieting Syrup to their babies to keep them calm during the mothers' long absences.

Imported from the East as a brown granular powder, the drug was mixed into tinctures—the most common being the reddish brown laudanum—which were easily available from the local apothecary. Some people used laudanum as a cheaper substitute for alcohol. There was a high demand for it in industrial centers such as Lancashire and Yorkshire as well as in London. One medical report described the situation: "There was not a village in all that region round but could show at least one shop and its counter loaded with the little laudanum-vials, even to the hundreds, for the accommodation of customers retiring from the workshops on Saturday night."

As the years passed, Coleridge's emotional state mirrored his physical misery. He conceived of several literary projects but seemed unable to carry them through. His professional failures were exacerbated by personal ones. He had trapped himself in a loveless marriage and had no regular income, with the exception of a small annuity from his patrons, to support his wife and children. By 1808, he was unable to endure his home life any longer and separated from his wife. He went to live with the Wordsworths.

Seeking both purpose and income, Coleridge created a new periodical called *The Friend: A Literary, Moral, and Political Weekly Paper*. At its heart, it was a Romantic publication, urging people to turn inward to self-reflection and self-understanding. But Coleridge could not sustain the effort, and the periodical folded seven months before his break with Wordsworth. Over the next several years, Coleridge drifted from lodging to lodging, publishing little of importance. Then, unexpectedly, he found success in two arenas: the lecture hall and the theater.

To earn money, Coleridge gave a series of public lectures on Shakespeare and Milton that became classics in English criticism. One groundbreaking lecture dealt with his interpretation of *Hamlet*. To 18th-century critics such as Voltaire, Samuel Johnson, and Goethe, *Hamlet* was a distasteful work, with a hero whose motivation was inexplicable and whose madness had no substantial cause. Voltaire dismissed the play as "a monstrous farce, haphazardly scattered with terrible soliloquies."

But to Coleridge, Hamlet was an Everyman, an archetypal Romantic hero, torn by his great imaginative power and inner struggle. His soliloquies on suicide, revenge, betrayal, and death dealt with universal concerns, producing "a communion with the *heart*, that belongs to, or ought to belong, to all mankind."

Coleridge garnered further acclaim in October 1812, when the Theatre Royal, Drury Lane, asked permission to produce *Osorio*, a previously unstaged play he had written in 1797. *Osorio* had been chosen only after careful consideration. There was a limited market for serious new dramas in London since only two theaters, the Theatre Royal and Covent Garden, were licensed to stage them. (Other theaters were restricted to producing burlesques, pantomimes, musicals, and operas.) Few productions lasted more than a week.

Osorio, a melodramatic story of two brothers who love the same woman, teems with grand passion, attempted murder, and magical conjuring, and was a perfect fit for the times. Opening night of the play, retitled *Remorse: A Tragedy in Five Acts*, was well attended, the great number of high-class prostitutes soliciting in the theater's foyer a testament to the fashionableness of the occasion. The audience loved *Remorse*, applauding wildly, particularly after the highly staged sorcery scene, which, said a critic, made "one half believe the enchantment which delighted our senses."

Remorse ran for an amazing 20 nights and became a part of the theater's spring repertoire. The script was published in book form and went through three editions. Provincial theatrical companies began performing it. The unprecedented success of *Remorse* proved a catalyst for London theater; many more plays were submitted and money willingly invested in future productions.

Medicine's Slow March

Global exploration extended England's boundaries to India, China, and Africa. It also brought back new diseases such as diphtheria, tuberculosis, typhus, typhoid, malaria, meningitis, and smallpox to a country still struggling to deal with its homegrown illnesses. Medical advancement was slow, hampered by uncooperative patients, misguided doctors, unsanitary conditions, and amoral opportunists.

Some diseases were welcomed by the sufferer. Considered a malady of the rich, the inflammation of the joints called gout was thought to be a prophylactic against other diseases. Consumption, or tuberculosis, was considered "a flattering complaint." Earnest young men paid pitiful court to dying women, whose souls supposedly emerged as their bodies wasted away.

Many upper-crust physicians specialized in the treatment of less dire female ailments, which were callously lumped under the term hysteria. They ran the gamut from menstrual problems to fainting spells brought on by tight corsets. Doctors freely prescribed laudanum, emetics, and purgatives for these complaints.

Infections were often caused by unsterile conditions in the

Using a lancet like the one above, Edward Jenner injects live cowpox cells into his first recipient, a young boy *(right)*, giving him immunity to the rampant smallpox. Jenner had observed that milkmaids, who worked with livestock, were immune to smallpox after having "Cow Pox."

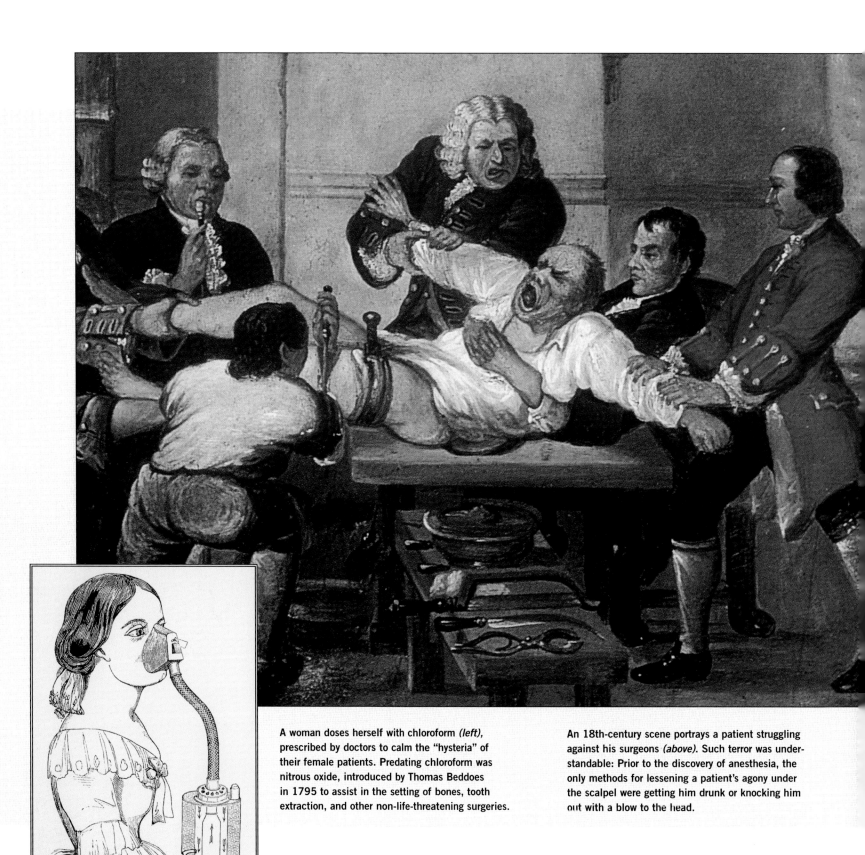

A woman doses herself with chloroform *(left)*, prescribed by doctors to calm the "hysteria" of their female patients. Predating chloroform was nitrous oxide, introduced by Thomas Beddoes in 1795 to assist in the setting of bones, tooth extraction, and other non-life-threatening surgeries.

An 18th-century scene portrays a patient struggling against his surgeons *(above)*. Such terror was understandable: Prior to the discovery of anesthesia, the only methods for lessening a patient's agony under the scalpel were getting him drunk or knocking him out with a blow to the head.

sickroom and could kill as readily as the original illness. Surgical instruments, bandages, and physicians' hands were all washed in water from the Thames, which contained raw sewage. Such filth precipitated a lengthy cholera epidemic that was not quelled until companies were forced by law to replace waste pipes in 1850.

In spite of the ghastly conditions, medical advancements were made during the 18th and 19th centuries. In 1785, digitalis, in the form of the foxglove plant, was found to cure cases of congestive heart failure. Edward Jenner pioneered a vaccination for smallpox in 1796. Adding fresh limes to their diet eliminated scurvy in the ranks of sailors of the British navy in 1795. René Laënnec created the stethoscope in 1816 from a simple flared tube.

Surgery also advanced. In the mid-18th century, William Hunter established a school offering formal instruction in anatomy to surgeons. As more doctors practiced the procedures, more cadavers were required for academic dissection. Local prisons were able to supply a few fresh corpses on execution days, but as the number of students grew, this source proved inadequate.

In 1820, William Burke and William Hare, who were owners of a boardinghouse, began selling the bodies of deceased boarders to surgeries. To create volume sales, the two hastened their boarders along by suffocating them in their beds and selling the bodies quickly. But medical students began noticing that their cadavers had once been healthy folk, free of discernible disease. Burke and Hare's scheme was revealed to the authorities, and the two were tried and hanged.

Progress in surgical methods continued, however, and in 1847, James Young Simpson championed the use of chloroform as an anesthetic. But the era's biggest breakthrough in surgical technique, Joseph Lister's proof of the value of antiseptics in preventing infection, would not come for another 30 years.

A furtive trio of graverobbers stuffs a corpse into a bag for easy transport to an anatomy school. Anatomy professors paid as much as £40 per body in the late 18th century, which encouraged such late-night escapades. The purchase of iron coffins became popular among families who wished to safeguard their loved ones' remains.

In the summer of 1815, Coleridge made another significant contribution with his *Biographia Literaria,* a discussion of his thoughts on the nature of poetry and the poet and a critique of Wordsworth's poems. At times rambling and uneven, it nevertheless came to be considered a great work of literary criticism.

But all of these successes played out against a backdrop of self-disgust and anguish as the writer's drug addiction worsened. In 1816 a desperate Coleridge traveled from London to the village of Highgate, three miles north, to meet Dr. James Gillman. Coleridge's own physician, Joseph Adams, had written Gillman to arrange the interview. "A very learned . . . gentleman," a discreet Adams explained, "wishes to fix himself in the house of some medical gentleman, who will have courage to refuse him any laudanum."

Both were being published for the first time at the urging of Lord Byron. Coleridge sent a note to Murray, asking him to "dispatch a Porter with the enclosed note [to an apothecary] who is to wait for an answer." Murray should pack up what the porter brought back with the proofs he was sending to Coleridge.

Fortunately, Gillman soon found out and put a stop to that ploy, and Coleridge's consumption of the drug was gradually reduced. Although the writer never completely stopped taking opium and still smuggled in extra doses at times, his overall use remained low. As a result, for the first time in several years, Coleridge was able to write regularly. Until his death in 1834, the grateful Coleridge continued to reside with the doctor who had given him, and his career, new life.

"*Few, as I soon discovered, were more impetuous in argumentative conversation.*"

Coleridge's manner and conversation captivated Gillman, who initially had been leery of the whole proposition. The men talked for two hours, leaving the doctor feeling "almost spellbound, without desire of release." Finally they agreed that the writer would move in three days later. Immediately after his departure, however, Coleridge sent Gillman a brutally frank letter of warning. His need for opium, he wrote, would force him into "*Evasion,* and the cunning of a specific madness." Furthermore, the servants "must receive absolute commands from you on no account to fetch anything for me."

Gillman found Coleridge true to his word. An early scheme by the writer to smuggle laudanum into his new home involved London publisher John Murray, who in 1816 was getting ready to publish Coleridge's poems "Kubla Khan" and "Christabel."

Coleridge had come to be admired by a younger generation of Romantic poets, which included not only Lord Byron but also Percy Bysshe Shelley. In October of 1810, the same month Coleridge and Wordsworth's friendship was coming to an end, 18-year-old Shelley, heir to a baronetcy in Sussex, was sent to Oxford University to study.

Oxford was one of England's most prominent universities. Yet in 1810 it was not so much a place of higher learning as it was a finishing school. The quality of the teaching was low; only a decade before had Oxford, founded in the 1200s, begun holding real examinations for degrees.

Percy Bysshe Shelley's father, Timothy, escorted his son to the university and introduced him to the proprietors of Slatter & Munday, Oxford booksellers and printers. The proud father told

them, "My son here has a literary turn; he is already an author, and do pray indulge him in his printing freaks." Indeed Bysshe, as his family called him, had already published a novel entitled *Zastrozzi,* which was a Gothic tale of passion, betrayal, and bloodshed, and a book of embarrassingly juvenile ballads and lyrics written with Elizabeth Shelley, one of his four younger sisters.

Writing was not young Shelley's only passion. Before entering Oxford, he had read William Godwin's *Political Justice,* a rejection of conventional government and other institutions. According to Godwin, the inherent power of such organizations to control people leads to tyranny. Establishing small self-sustaining communities, on the other hand, would foster unfettered intellectual inquiry and allow society to reach a state of

Two 19th-century students amuse themselves in their Oxford room. During the previous century, England's universities had lost their prestigious reputations, and although less well-to-do young men still enrolled to prepare for a university or church career, their wealthy classmates simply enjoyed spending money and carousing. Many upper-class students, including Shelley, never completed the three-year undergraduate curriculum.

THE ELEGANT DANDY

The early 1800s saw a revolution in men's clothing. In place of 18th-century wigs, makeup, silks, velvets, and bright colors came an understated elegance championed by renowned dandy George "Beau" Brummell. Under his influence, the cut of a man's coat became more important than its ability to attract attention. Pants changed as well. After the French Revolution, gentlemen had replaced their knee breeches with the formerly lower-class trousers. Brummell added a strap so that trousers could be worn tighter to show off well-proportioned calves. He also introduced black-and-white formal attire. As an accessory, a well-dressed man carried a walking cane.

The more exaggerated aspects of their dress made dandies the brunt of satirists *(above)*. Cartoons featured pants so tight that the wearer could not sit down, waists cinched in by corsets, and high starched cravats that restricted head movement.

Brummell's trendsetting ended in 1814, when he fell from the prince regent's grace and out of social favor. One of his ideas, fortunately, stayed in vogue: He insisted that men should bathe, shave, and change their clothes daily.

contented anarchy, where crime would disappear and wealth would be distributed equally. Godwin's belief that politics is founded on a morality defined in utilitarian rather than religious terms justified Shelley's own unswerving belief in political possibility and his rejection of orthodox religion, and he heartily embraced Godwin's secular philosophy.

At Oxford Shelley made the acquaintance of the like-minded Thomas Hogg. "Few, as I soon discovered," Hogg recalled of Shelley, "were more impetuous in argumentative conversation." And few had more eclectic interests. Hogg described Shelley's rooms as a maelstrom of "books, boots, papers, shoes, philosophical instruments, clothes, pistols, linen, crockery, ammunition, and phials innumerable." In this clutter, he also spied "an electrical machine, an air pump, the galvanic trough, a solar microscope, and large glass jars and receivers."

The following spring, the impetuous Shelley printed up a little pamphlet titled *The Necessity of Atheism,* a composite of his and Hogg's writings in which they inquired into the principles of religious belief. Intending to spark a debate, they observed that logical argument ("of necessity") seemed to point to atheism. A few days later, Shelley was called before angry college dons.

"Are you the author of this book?" one of the school officials demanded.

Noting that the man seemed "resolved to punish" him if he said yes, Shelley responded, "If you can prove that it is [my work], produce your evidence. It is neither just nor lawful to interrogate me in such a case and for such a purpose. Such proceedings would become a court of inquisitors, but not free men in a free country."

Shelley was summarily expelled. Hogg, when told of the news, went before the dons himself and suffered the same fate. Shelley's father was furious at the young man for having been "sent down" from Oxford University. But through the intercession of an uncle, an agreement between father and son was eventually reached. Bysshe was granted an allowance of £200 per year; in return he agreed to take up a profession (though he never did). A frugal and practical person could have made do quite well on this, but neither trait was Shelley's strong suit. He would spend the rest of his life skirting financial disaster, always managing to persuade bankers and others to lend him money against his expected inheritance.

The 19-year-old Shelley once again defied convention in August when he eloped to Scotland with 16-year-old Harriet Westbrook, a school friend of his sister Elizabeth's. Though he did not believe in marriage, he had decided to wed Harriet for several reasons: He loved her and knew she would suffer more than he if they lived together out of wedlock; she was unhappy in her present circumstances; and the marriage defied his father, who had said he would not tolerate such a misalliance.

The groom then persuaded Hogg to join him and his young bride in Edinburgh, thus setting up the first of what would be a series of *ménages à trois* . . . or *quatre* . . . or more. Sharing his home with several friends seemed to be the poet's preferred household arrangement. He firmly believed in free love, a belief he wrote about in a later poem entitled *Epipsychidion:*

I never was attached to that great sect,
Whose doctrine is, that each one should select
Out of the crowd a mistress or a friend,
And all the rest, though fair and wise, commend
To cold oblivion . . .

In January 1812, having recently learned that his idol William Godwin was still alive, Shelley wrote to him, describing in one letter the effect *Political Justice* had had on him. "Till then

I had existed in an ideal world; now I found that in this universe of ours was enough to excite the interest of the heart, enough to employ the discussions of Reason. I beheld in short that I had duties to perform."

One of the "duties" involved raising people's consciousness. He went so far as to row out into the Bristol Channel to disseminate his *Declaration of Rights* (patterned on the American and French examples) to the world by stuffing the leaflets in bottles or setting them adrift in homemade boats.

By now Harriet's older sister Eliza had become a permanent member of the Shelley household, and the trio went to stay in the remote village of Lynmouth. Money was again a problem, but the poet charmed his landlady into lending him some. He had an ability to win over women of any station. In part this may have been due to his manner: He took women as seriously as he would any man. However, with abundant, curly hair and large, deep blue eyes, he was also angelically attractive.

Shelley then moved his household to London, where he finally met William Godwin. The philosopher's finances were in the process of deteriorating rapidly, and although Shelley was scarcely better off, he could, as always, raise money against his future inheritance. This he now did, considering it a privilege to support so great a man.

Godwin introduced Shelley to one John Newton, who converted the poet to vegetarianism. Shelley had never been one to pay much attention to meals, in any case, subsisting largely on bread, honey, raisins, fruit, and tea. Indeed, Thomas Hogg had often complained of the meager pickings at the Shelley table. Now Shelley embraced vegetarianism, even incorporating the concept into *Queen Mab,* an allegorical tale cum political polemic he was then writing.

When the poem was finished, Thomas Hookham, the poet's publisher, refused to publish it for fear of being prosecuted. As Shelley's wife wrote to a friend, "It is too much against every existing establishment." But Hookham printed 250 copies at Shelley's expense in 1813, and about 70 copies were privately distributed. The intellectual positions he set forth in *Queen Mab* would emerge again, more powerfully, in his masterpiece *Prometheus Unbound* (1820):

> The loathsome mask has fallen, the Man remains,—
> Sceptreless, free, uncircumscribed,—but man:
> Equal, unclassed, tribeless and nationless,
> Exempt from awe, worship, degree, the King
> Over himself.

The same year that *Queen Mab* was published, Percy Bysshe Shelley became a father: His wife Harriet gave birth to a daughter, Ianthe, in June 1813. The poet's ever-dicey finances now grew even more precarious. He was soon being hounded by creditors and had to get as far from London as possible. During one of these sojourns he made the acquaintance of a mother and daughter, the Boinvilles, whose company he began to find much more pleasant than that of his wife. Harriet, upset by her husband's unabashed courting of the daughter, departed for the country with the baby.

A few weeks later, with his marriage clearly in decline, Shelley met 16-year-old Mary Godwin, the philosopher's daughter by feminist writer Mary Wollstonecraft. Soon Shelley was seeking Mary at her favorite retreat, her mother's grave in St. Pancras churchyard. By early July 1814, the two had declared their love. William Godwin was adamantly opposed to the situation, and Shelley's wife arrived at the Godwins' house, pregnant again and visibly distressed.

The Sporting Life

During the Romantic era, competitive sports were enormously popular throughout England. Elite preparatory schools and universities such as Eton and Oxford, where Shelley studied, included sports in the curriculum to cultivate perseverance and build sound moral character. Rich and poor alike delighted in watching sports, cheering on their favorite local football or cricket teams, and enjoying individual competitions such as boxing and horse racing.

Cricket, England's most popular team sport, may have originated as early as the 13th century among townspeople who competed against neighboring villagers. By the early 1700s, it was not unusual for the 11-member teams to include noblemen, gentlemen, and clergymen playing alongside butchers, cobblers, and tinkers. In the 19th century, cricket became increasingly fashionable, the ranks of its amateur stars boasting such notables as William Ward, a member of Parliament and director of the Bank of England. Women played cricket as well. An 1811 match featured two female teams, whose ages ranged from 14 to 50.

More brutal than cricket, though no less fascinating, was boxing. "Foreigners can scarcely understand how we can squeeze pleasure out of this pastime; the luxury of hard

In the 1790s, aristocrats play a cricket match, dressed typically in white clothing and top hats *(center)*. At left, a 19th-century batsman waits for the pitch.

Two English gentlemen practice their sparring skills in Jackson's Rooms, a popular boxing school in London, in the 1820s. The protective muffles, or boxing gloves, that the men are wearing were not made mandatory in the ring until the late 19th century.

blows given or received, the great joy of the ring," noted writer William Hazlitt. In 1810, thousands of fans stood in a cold December rain as the great Tom Cribb knocked out his opponent, Tom Molineaux, in 33 rounds. Though boxing had been ruled illegal 60 years before, local officials allowed the sport to continue because the wealthy supported it. Aristocratic patrons proudly drove their favored boxers to ringside in coaches and studied the "manly art of self-defense" themselves from former champion "Gentleman" John Jackson at his London school. The poet Lord Byron dubbed Jackson "Emperor of Pugilism."

Horse racing was another rough sport popular in all segments of society. It was controlled, however, almost exclusively by the rich, who owned most of the horses and the racetracks. Racing's governing body, the Jockey Club, drafted laws, set rules of conduct, and oversaw the "studbook," an elite registry of thoroughbred horses. For the rich, the grand racing event of the year was the royal meeting at Ascot, established by Queen Anne in 1711, while the lower classes flocked to the Epsom Derby.

No matter what the sport, the English loved to bet on the outcome, whether it be a laborer staking a day's pay or an aristocrat wagering enormous sums. Gambling proved to be a problem, often leading to corruption and violence. Horse racing's Jockey Club had been formed in the 1750s by wealthy horse owners whose concerns about corruption led to reforms. Cricket, overseen by the Marylebone Cricket Club, banned bookmakers from the games in 1825. Boxing, too, had its regulations. But corrupt practices such as paying a boxer to lose grew so common that interest in the sport—which was also increasingly condemned for its brutality—had dwindled by the mid-19th century.

At York in 1804, 22-year-old Alicia Thornton takes the lead. Her horse broke down near the race's end, and 150 years passed before another woman raced in England.

In the early hours of July 28, the lovers, accompanied at the last minute by Mary's stepsister Jane Clairmont (later usually called Claire), ran off to the Continent.

For just over a month, the trio wandered through France and Switzerland, managing somehow on virtually no money. Early on, Shelley sold his watch and chain to keep them going. By fall, however, they were forced to head home. Over the next several months, Shelley made the rounds of friends, solicitors, and moneylenders in an effort to scare up enough to live on and to continue his promised financial support of William Godwin. The philosopher, meanwhile, coldly refused to see his daughters or Shelley, despite continuing to accept the poet's money. A vicious rumor began to circulate that William Godwin had sold his daughters to Shelley for £1,500.

Before long, Shelley's creditors were again hounding him, and he went into hiding. Mary Godwin and Shelley would meet clandestinely in coffeehouses. Shelley was so distracted that he could do no writing. "Do you think Wordsworth could have written such poetry," he asked plaintively, "if he had ever had dealings with money lenders?"

On November 30, Harriet Shelley gave birth to a son, and just after the New Year of 1815 the poet learned that his grandfather had died. Timothy Shelley now settled his son's outstanding debts and gave him an annuity of £1,000, of which a fifth was sent directly to Harriet and the children.

Shelley's friend Thomas Hogg was now spending considerable time with Mary Godwin, whose own pregnancy often kept her at home while, to her irritation, Shelley went out and about with her sister. An ambiguous sort of affair developed between Godwin and Hogg. In March, when her premature baby died four days after its birth, Godwin sent for him: "My dearest Hogg my baby is dead—will you come as soon as you can? . . . You are so calm a creature & Shelley is afraid of a fever from the milk—for I am no longer a mother now." Godwin was willing to submit to Hogg's milder attentions, though she fended off physical consummation. Her acquiescence to him seemed to be driven mainly by her desire to please Shelley by following his principles of communal love. The poet, for his part, outwardly promoted the affair but became ill with anxiety.

Shelley regained his health in late August and September, when he and Mary Godwin spent several weeks in Bishopsgate, west of London, for once without any extra people in the household. In this rare tranquil state he began writing *Alastor, or the Spirit of Solitude,* an autobiographical fantasy that was a major departure from the polemics of *Queen Mab.* Published in January 1816, it drew generally hostile reviews—"wild and specious, untangible and incoherent as a dream"—but later reviewers regarded it as Shelley's first mature poetic achievement.

The year 1816 would prove memorable for several other reasons. In January, Mary Godwin gave birth to a baby boy, named William. Then, that summer, Shelley met the infamous George Gordon, Lord Byron, who was living in exile in Geneva. Godwin and Shelley had been urged to go to Geneva by Claire Clairmont, who had managed to introduce herself to Byron earlier in the year and had become pregnant by him.

The two poets liked each other immediately. The next few months were for them as mutually stimulating as the Alfoxden year had been for Wordsworth and Coleridge. They spent hours together sailing, though Shelley did not know how to swim, and gathered together in the evening at one another's rented homes. One night at Byron's villa,

Reflecting the Romantic fascination with the exotic, George Gordon, Lord Byron, *(right)* poses in an Albanian costume in 1813. Three years later, he fled England under a cloud of scandal and rented Villa Diodati *(above)* on a hill overlooking Lake Geneva. In Geneva, he met Percy Bysshe Shelley, who lived with his extended family in a more modest home just down the hill from Byron's villa. The poets became friends, and in the evenings their two households often dined together.

the company decided that each of them should write a ghost story. In her tale, Mary Godwin wove together two of Shelley's favorite themes—the terror of the supernatural and the potential power of science—and produced *Frankenstein.* Written when she was just 18 and published two years later, the story would prove to have a more widespread and long-lasting public impact than anything else she ever wrote—and would be more popular than anything produced by either Shelley or Byron.

On returning to England in the fall, the Shelley-Godwin household was buffeted by two suicides. In October, Mary's half sister Fanny, long feeling depressed and oppressed living in her stepfather's house, took an overdose of laudanum. Then, in December, Harriet Shelley's body was dragged from Serpentine Lake in London. Hoping to gain custody of his daughter and son by making himself more respectable, the poet wed Mary Godwin. The ploy did not succeed, however, and early in 1817 the children were awarded to the care of a doctor. "No words can express the anguish he felt when his elder children were torn from him," Mary later wrote.

That year the number of children in the Shelley household increased nonetheless, with the birth in January 1817 of Allegra, the daughter of Clairmont and Byron, and in September of Clara, the daughter of Bysshe and Mary. In March 1818, Shelley transported his household of three babies and four women (including two nurses for the children) to Italy, choosing that country in part because Byron was there and they would be taking Allegra to him. Percy Bysshe Shelley would never set foot in England again.

AN EXTRAORDINARY REGARD

"They have an extraordinary Regard in England for young Children," a Frenchman observed, noting that the French "correct our Children as soon as they are capable of reasoning." Indeed, the English had replaced the idea of children as sinful from birth and in need of restraint with that of children as naturally innocent and inclined to goodness. English artists presented this view of childhood in poetry and paintings *(left)*.

English parents also began to place more emphasis on education. Instructional toys and books, such as *Educational Cards for the Amusement of Youth,* sold well. Some children started their education at an early age. John Stuart Mill studied Greek at age three; other child prodigies could recite long passages of the Bible or Shakespeare. Lord Byron, who had been an avid reader in his youth, felt that his daughter Allegra should have been reading at age four and sent her to a convent to begin her formal education.

The next four years were eventful, productive, and, from Mary Shelley's perspective especially, unutterably tragic. In September 1818, year-old Clara took ill and died in the hallway of a Venetian inn while her father searched in vain for a doctor. The resulting strain on the relationship between little Clara's parents was compounded by Claire Clairmont's distress over giving up her daughter to Byron's indifferent care. Her brother-in-law had insisted on the action, however, because he considered it better for Allegra and because the infant's presence in his household added fuel to the rumors of a Shelley harem. All these events weighed heavily on Shelley, whose despair emerged in his poetry, in *Stanzas Written in Dejection, near Naples:*

> Alas! I have nor hope nor health,
> Nor peace within nor calm around,
> Nor that content surpassing wealth
> The sage in meditation found,
> And walked with inward glory crowned—
> Nor fame, nor power, nor love, nor leisure.
> Others I see whom these surround—
> Smiling they live, and call life pleasure;—
> To me that cup has been dealt in another measure.

Worse was in store. In June 1819, while the family was in Rome, three-and-a-half-year-old William died after a brief illness. Mary, who was pregnant again, recorded the bitter harvest of her life with her husband: "We have now lived five years together; and if all the events of the five years were blotted out, I might be happy; but to have won, and then cruelly to have lost, the associations of four years is not an accident to which the human mind can bend without much suffering." In November, Mary gave birth to another son, Percy Florence (who would be their only surviving child), and slowly began to recover her spirits.

Over the next two and a half years, Percy Bysshe Shelley would complete some dozen works of prose and poetry, including *Prometheus Unbound, The Cenci, The Masque of Anarchy, A Defence of Poetry, Letter to Maria Gisborne, Epipsychidion,* and *Adonais.* He worked wherever they were living, with houseguests and visitors coming and going. There were transient obsessions or flirtations and the continual tribulations of his passionate friendships and unconventional approach to love.

When the Shelleys settled in Pisa, some new friends became part of their circle, including Edward and Jane Williams, friends of a cousin, Tom Medwin; the Greek prince Aléxandros Mavrokordátos, who gave Mary lessons in Greek; and Edward Trelawny, a Cornish adventurer who was a friend of the Williamses'. Byron was also a member of the literary cadre that Mary described as "a little nest of singing birds." In 1822, Bysshe conceived the idea that Romantic essayist and poet Leigh Hunt should move his family from England to Pisa so that Hunt and Byron could start a literary and political magazine to be called *The Liberal.* While they waited for the Hunts to arrive, Percy Bysshe Shelley and Edward Williams ordered a sailboat built, which arrived in May.

At about this time, Mary suffered a miscarriage and became severely depressed. Her mood was not helped by the cramped quarters they were inhabiting: The Shelley family and the Williamses shared Casa Magni, a small house on a remote beach. "Their servants and mine quarrel like cats and dogs," Mary complained in a letter to a friend. In addition, her husband began to have nightmares and waking hallucinations. In one, a naked child resembling Claire Clairmont and Lord Byron's daughter, Allegra, who had recently died, rose out of the sea clapping her hands. In another, the Williamses, bloodied and injured, came into his room to warn him that the house was collapsing; when he ran to tell his wife, he dreamed that he strangled her. These apparitions were ominous enough at the time; in retrospect they seemed like premonitions.

In mid-June, the Hunts arrived in Genoa and set out down the coast toward Livorno, where they and their six children would be staying with Byron in a rented villa. On July 1, Percy Bysshe Shelley and Edward Williams, accompanied only by an 18-year-old English boatboy named Charles Vivian, sailed across the Gulf of Spezia south to Livorno to welcome the Hunts and smooth the initial meeting with Byron.

The men were expected home on Monday the 8th. When Monday proved stormy, Mary Shelley and Jane Williams were sure that their husbands had delayed their departure. No boat appeared over the next two days, however, and now the women expected that Friday's mail would bring word that the men had decided to stay in Livorno for business reasons. But Friday's mail turned up only a letter from Leigh Hunt asking if the travelers had made it home safely, since they had departed as a storm was brewing. For the next week, searchers combed the beaches. On the 19th of July, Trelawny brought the dreadful news that the bodies of the three lost sailors had washed up on the beach between Viareggio and Massa.

Adhering to Italian quarantine law, which required that corpses washed ashore be covered with lime and interred at the spot where they were found, the authorities had buried the drowned men on the beach. But Mary Shelley wanted her husband's body to be laid to rest in the Protestant Cemetery in Rome, beside their son William. Thus, to fulfill Mary's wishes, Trelawny, Hunt, and Byron found themselves a few weeks later pulling their friend's putrefied corpse from the sands.

The sun was fierce, the sand a furnace. Trelawny started the funeral pyre while Hunt remained in the carriage, huddled in misery. Byron flung himself into the sea, swimming out to his boat, the *Bolivar,* which was anchored nearby. There was no sound but the lapping of waves and the roar of the flames. The body refused to burn easily, and the mourning friends had to keep the fire going for four hours.

When at last the poet's ashes were gathered, the three returned to Viareggio to eat a spare meal and consume a substantial quantity of wine. Hunt later recalled the drunken survivors' journey onward to Pisa with a feeling of shame: "We sang, we laughed, we shouted. I even felt a gayety the more shocking, because it was real and a relief."

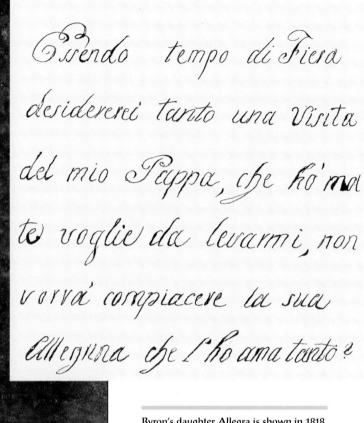

Caro il mio Pappa

Essendo tempo di Fiera desidererei tanto una Visita del mio Pappa, che hò molte voglie da levarmi, non vorrà compiacere la sua Allegrina che l'ho ama tanto?

Byron's daughter Allegra is shown in 1818, around the time she went to live with him. In 1821, someone at the convent where she was staying sent Byron a letter *(above)*, in which the four-year-old asked him to take her to a fair. He did not respond, and she died the following year. "While she lived, her existence never seemed necessary to my happiness," wrote Byron, "but no sooner did I lose her, than it appeared to me as if I could not live without her."

In a highly romanticized painting of Shelley's funeral pyre, Byron, Edward Trelawny, and Leigh Hunt keep a vigil as the poet's intact corpse is cremated. In reality the body, exhumed from the beach, was badly decomposed, and neither Hunt nor Byron could bear to watch the cremation. Strangely, Shelley's heart did not burn, and Trelawny had it preserved in wine. Eventually Mary Shelley (above) took possession of it.

It had been six years since Byron had first met Shelley in Geneva—and six years since Byron had fled England to escape scandal and debt. Both scandal and debt were common conditions in his family. George Gordon Byron, born in 1788, came from a long line of rakes, spendthrifts, and eccentrics. His granduncle William Byron, known as the Wicked Lord, killed a man in a dispute, then secured his freedom from prison by paying a fine. He spent money recklessly on building such structures as a miniature castle in which he held lavish parties and two lakeside forts from which he launched mock naval battles. He eventually ran his estate into ruinous debt. William's brother was a notorious rake known as Foul-weather Jack; Foul-weather's son, called Mad Jack, was even wilder and more irresponsible. Mad Jack would, without a qualm, abandon his wife and son, George Gordon, to the fates.

That son, born with a deformed foot that would always make him feel like an outsider, spent the first years of his life in Aberdeen, Scotland, his mother's homeland, before succeeding to his granduncle's baronetcy in 1798. (All other heirs, including George's father, had predeceased William.) Byron and his mother moved south to Newstead, England, where the sadly encumbered and run-down ancestral home was located. In 1805, he left Newstead to study at Cambridge.

A voracious reader of English classics, biographies, historical works, and modern poetry, Byron enjoyed life at the university. As a peer, he was not required to take examinations and enjoyed proudly walking the grounds in his nobleman's black gown with gold embroidery. Following family tradition, he lived beyond his means, and by the time he turned 20, in 1808, he owed his many creditors some £5,000.

Unable to stay at Cambridge because of his outstanding bills, Byron chose to live in London and write. He had already pub-

lished two books of poems. Embittered by the negative reviews, particularly in the *Edinburgh Review,* of the second book, *Hours of Idleness,* and by other real or imagined slights, Byron turned his latest literary effort into a biting and vitriolic satire entitled *English Bards and Scotch Reviewers.* In it, he insulted several well-known writers, including William Wordsworth and Walter Scott, as well as prominent members of the nobility. Many people were appalled by the book's viciousness, and Byron himself would come to regret publishing it.

With *English Bards,* Byron had once again become a victim of his own emotions. Throughout his life, he cycled between periods of manic, high-energy grandiosity and moods of depression and paranoia. His weight fluctuated with his mood. In times of lethargy and dissipation, he grew "bloated, and sallow," his knuckles "lost in fat," as one acquaintance described it. During manic periods he would become obsessed with his weight, exercise fanatically, and grow skeletal on a meager diet of vinegar, water, and a bit of rice.

In July 1809, hounded by creditors, Byron left England and spent two years abroad. He was beguiled by Lisbon's beautiful harbor, which was surrounded by terraced gardens and orange groves. Here he swam across the Tagus River, a feat less renowned but more arduous than his swimming of the Hellespont, a strait in modern-day Turkey, some 10 months later. (Self-conscious because of his deformity, he always wore long trousers when swimming.) From Portugal, he journeyed to Spain, Malta, Sicily, Albania, Greece, and the Ottoman Empire. On his return to England in 1811, he transformed his experiences—the rigors and exhilaration of living close to nature, the breath-

A fanciful painting portrays Byron resting in the house of a fisherman after swimming the Hellespont, a feat he felt would assure his fame. "I plume myself on this achievement," Byron wrote, "more than I could possibly do on any kind of glory, political, poetical, or rhetorical." He frequently mentioned the swim in his letters, especially those to his mother, who had taunted him cruelly about his crippled foot.

taking scenery, and the exotic customs of the mysterious East—into the early cantos of *Childe Harold's Pilgrimage.*

The book was published in March 1812; the timing could not have been more auspicious. The London season, which began when Parliament opened for a new session in January or February, was already under way. The nobility and gentry were flocking to the capital from their country estates, ready to enjoy a whirlwind of social events, including dinner parties, soirees, balls, and sporting contests, and to marry off their eligible daughters. Many of these sophisticates had read the still-notorious *English Bards* and were eager to see what else Byron might write.

The subject matter of *Childe Harold* drew new readers as well. There was a current fascination with exotic locales. And the poem introduced a new type of literary figure that was appealing to the Romantics: the tortured hero and noble loner. Though an egoist, the childe—a term applied to those of noble birth—was also a man of deep feeling, who mourned for a lost love and fought against oppression.

Childe Harold became the most talked about book of the season. Society, which identified Byron with his protagonist, showered the handsome poet with invitations, and young women wrote him love letters. Among his admirers was Caroline Lamb, who wrote in her diary, "That beautiful pale face is my fate." So it would prove, as the two embarked upon one of England's most scandalous affairs.

Caroline Lamb, the wife of nobleman and member of Parliament William Lamb, was charming, capricious, and moody. She could slip quickly from depression to gaiety and was subject to terrible rages. She reveled in defying convention, and she had no shame in her pursuit of Byron. She wrote him love letters, offering him not only herself but her jewels as well. If he attended a ball to which she had not been invited, she waited for him on the street outside. She also enjoyed dressing up, privately, in the silks and laces of a page for Byron, who seemed taken with her in this boyish disguise. (The poet had long admired the charms of both women and men.) But by the summer, Byron had begun to weary of his admirer's wild emotions. Desperate, Lamb sought any means to win him back.

One day in late July, a young man, whose face and figure were muffled by layers of clothing, appeared on Byron's doorstep. Ushered in to see the poet, the mysterious visitor threw off the heavy outer garments and revealed herself to be Caroline Lamb, dressed as a page. A friend of Byron's who was present was shocked by this scandalous behavior. Byron himself urgently sought to persuade Lamb to go into a bedroom and change into women's clothes, which he would have one of his female

My Sister—my sweet Sister—if a name
Dearer and purer were—it should be thine.
Mountains and Seas divide us—but I claim
No tears—but tenderness to answer mine:
Go where I will, to me thou art the same—
A loved regret which I would not resign—
There yet are two things in my destiny
A world to roam through—and a home with thee.

Rumors that the half brother and sister were having an incestuous relationship began to be whispered about, and Byron's financial condition continued to deteriorate. In April 1816, he fled

"*I cannot easily describe the emotions which such a scene excited.*"

servants provide. Lamb finally did so but then snatched up a knife and threatened to stab herself. Byron grabbed her and wrestled it away. Eventually, Lamb allowed herself to be escorted back to her home by Byron's friend.

The affair with Lamb over, at least as far as he was concerned, Byron decided to marry, with the hope of rescuing himself from financial ruin. But his marriage to Annabella Milbanke in January 1815 seemed doomed from the beginning. After the wedding, Byron was disappointed to learn that Annabella was not the heiress that he had assumed she was; besides, his deepest affections already seemed to lie elsewhere—with his half sister, Augusta. Augusta, four years older than her brother, was a kind of female version of Byron, with chestnut hair, an expressive mouth, and large eyes. From exile he would address some of his tenderest lines of poetry to her.

England once again, abandoning his wife and the daughter, Augusta Ada, who had been born to them five months before.

The poet drifted wherever fancy drew him, determined that if society thought him amoral and promiscuous he would defiantly confirm the low opinion. In Venice, he boasted, he had bedded at least 200 women; Shelley had been appalled. Shelley wrote to a mutual friend, "He allows fathers & mothers to bargain with him for their daughters," apparently a common practice at the time, at least in Venice.

Byron continued to write. In 1819 he finished the third canto of his poetic work *Don Juan,* a picaresque satire based on events in his own life. When part of the poem was published two years later, his memorable lines to "the isles of Greece" would inspire support in England for the Greek uprising that year against their Turkish oppressors.

Lady Caroline Lamb poses dressed as a page in 1813, the year after she met Byron. She described him as "mad, bad, and dangerous to know"; he called her "a little volcano." Their affair was brief, her recklessness and possessiveness turning Byron against her. In revenge, she cast him as the villain in her 1816 Gothic novel *Glenarvon*, a badly written bestseller.

The mountains look on Marathon—
And Marathon looks on the sea;
And musing there an hour alone,
I dream'd that Greece might still be free;
For standing on the Persian's grave,
I could not deem myself a slave.

In 1823, the London Greek Committee sought to convince Byron that his presence in Greece— along with any financial aid he could offer—would have an enormously positive impact. "If I go there," Byron said, "I shall do my best to civilize their mode of treating their prisoners." He also saw that going to Greece with the aim of promoting liberty might give him an opportunity to gain some glory, allowing him to hold his head up again—and perhaps return to England.

When Byron finally departed from Genoa, his small vessel, the *Hercules,* was crammed with livestock, four horses, a bulldog and a Newfoundland, enough medicine to supply a thousand men for a year, and chests of money: 10,000 Spanish pesetas and bills of exchange for £40,000 from England. For a while, it seemed that the grand adventure would lean toward the farcical. The boat was an unwieldy barge that wallowed along slowly, taking five days to reach Livorno. There, a handful of Greek "patriots" talked their way aboard and were soon squabbling among themselves. Byron shut himself up in his cabin.

Prince Mavrokordátos, the Greek patriot who had been Mary Shelley's language tutor, had returned to Greece and established a provisional government in Missolonghi, and he urged Byron to join him there. The poet's primary duty would be the administration of a promised loan from England meant for establishing, arming, and training the revolutionary army. Mavrokordátos wrote to Byron, begging him to come soon: "Be assured, My Lord, that it depends only on yourself to secure the destiny of Greece." Byron had no military experience and had always railed against war. Yet now he was preparing to return to Greece in the role of a military commander.

At length, on the morning of January 5, 1824, Byron arrived in Missolonghi, arrayed for the event in a scarlet regimental uniform he had borrowed from an officer in Italy. He was greeted with a 21-gun salute and cheering crowds, then escorted to a house where he met with Mavrokordátos and a number of other dignitaries. It was apparently an inspiring moment. "I cannot easily describe the emotions which such a scene excited," Byron's traveling companion Pietro Gamba wrote in his journal. "I could scarcely refrain from tears."

But Byron's own elation faded quickly in the face of reality. The town itself was little more than a collection of wretched huts for some 3,000 fishermen, situated near some stagnant lagoons. Narrow, muddy lanes reeked of human excrement. Cold rain fell incessantly. Now Byron's ordeal began. Even though his instructions from the London Greek Committee precluded engaging in military operations, people were looking to him to make decisions and plan strategy. Byron tried to assemble a brigade, with little success. Each morning a motley crew would assemble for rifle drill—but they had no weapons yet, and the drill instructor had not arrived. Mavrokordátos and Byron each began to suspect the other of plotting a takeover of command. The tension caused Byron to lose his temper even with Gamba, whom he trusted implicitly, and with his attractive young page, Loukas, with whom he was besotted.

On his birthday, January 22, Byron read aloud a poem he had written especially for the occasion, called "On This Day I Complete My Thirty-Sixth Year." In it, he seemed to declare that he would break the chains of desire he felt for Loukas—a passion he deemed unworthy—by seeking death: "A Soldier's Grave—for thee the best, / Then look around and choose thy ground / And take thy Rest."

But Byron did not die a soldier's death. What were to be his final days began in mid-February, when he had a convulsive fit that was probably brought on by a high fever. Then, although he seemed to rally from time to time, his health deteriorated over the next two months. On the morning of April 16, his two inexperienced doctors (who had been hired right out of medical school to save money) tried to bleed him; they had to make three attempts to open his veins and attach the leeches. Over the subsequent three days, Byron drifted in and out of consciousness, shivering and delirious, while around him the household degenerated into chaos. Late on the afternoon of Easter Sunday, Byron realized the end was near. He began crying out for his daughter Ada, whom he had not seen in eight years, and for his sister Augusta. When his voice failed him, he began muttering, trying to give instructions no one could understand. The following day, April 19, at 6:00 in the evening, he opened his eyes for a moment, closed them again—and was gone.

Two months later, his body was returned home to England and put on public view for two days. The funeral cortege included a strange procession: the empty carriages of the aristocratic families of London, people who had once flocked to court the dashing author of *Childe Harold's Pilgrimage* and who now refused to express anything more for him than the mere formality of mourning.

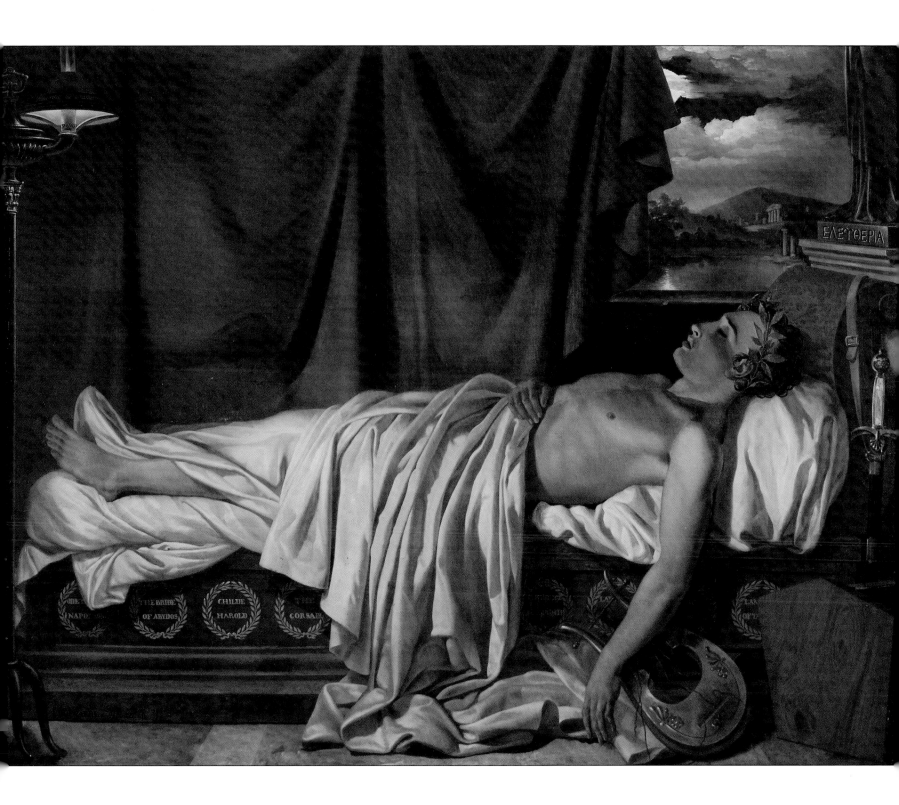

147

An Industrial Revolution

Although the ancient Egyptians identified steam as a source of power, it was not until the 18th and 19th centuries, when British engineers such as James Watt and George Stephenson introduced and then refined the steam engine, that the steam-powered Industrial Revolution began. Seemingly overnight, pristine country villages were transformed into industrial centers fouled with soot, noisy with clanging machinery, and crammed with workers who operated pumps, looms, and presses, all powered by steam.

But for the revolution to take hold, more than steam was necessary. Entrepreneurs with capital (much of it from overseas trade) and access to a steady supply of cheap raw materials and labor were also required. Nowhere were these ingredients more heavily concentrated than in Britain during the 19th century. New farming techniques, for example, had substantially increased yields, in turn contributing to an explosion of Britain's population, which grew from nine million to 18 million during the first half of the century. But the shift from rural to industrial life was not easy. Life in preindustrial Britain had been governed by the seasons; now the new industrial workers were at the mercy of factory owners and their machines, which ran day and night regardless of the weather.

Located near abundant coal and iron ore deposits and known for its production of fine cutlery, the prosperous northern town of Sheffield grew in population by 500 percent during the first half of the 19th century. Crowded with smokestacks and slums, Sheffield typified the dramatic changes in daily life that came with industrialization.

Mining for Coal

With a dizzying circularity that marked the age, the demand for coal to run the machinery that produced iron to build more engines in order to extract more coal to generate the steam that powered new factories increased exponentially. Between 1800 and 1846, output from coal mines in Britain climbed from 10 million to 44 million tons a year.

The pace for mine workers was killing. Shifts in the mines were often a grueling 12 to 13 hours a day, six days a week, though in one documented case, miners worked up to 39 continuous hours with neither food nor rest. Physically better able to fit themselves into confined spaces, women and children, some as young as four and five years old, worked in the mines alongside men, all toiling beneath the earth to the point of exhaustion.

Among the common perils miners faced on the job were collapsing ceilings, which gave way with no more warning than the crack of supporting timbers, and poisonous gases such as carbonic-acid gas, known as chokedamp. An even more dangerous gas was methane, or firedamp, which would explode when it was ignited by sparks from attempts to provide light in the pitch-black mines. Between 1835 and 1850, there were 643 recorded mine explosions caused by firedamp.

In 1842, Lord Ashley, who later became the earl of Shaftesbury, prevailed upon Parliament to enact reforms by recounting some of the many abuses the miners endured. Ashley told of one woman miner who had miscarried five times, and of Sarah Gooder, an eight-year-old miner who said of her work in the coal mines, "It scares me. I don't like being in the pit." Bucking stiff opposition from wealthy mine owners, Lord Ashley managed to get Parliament to pass laws prohibiting all women and girls and boys younger than 10 from working in the mines.

By about 1820, a steam engine such as the one below, powered by burning coal, would have been positioned at the pithead, or entrance, of a coal mine. These early steam engines were used to pump out water, enabling miners to dig deeper and reach the richest deposits.

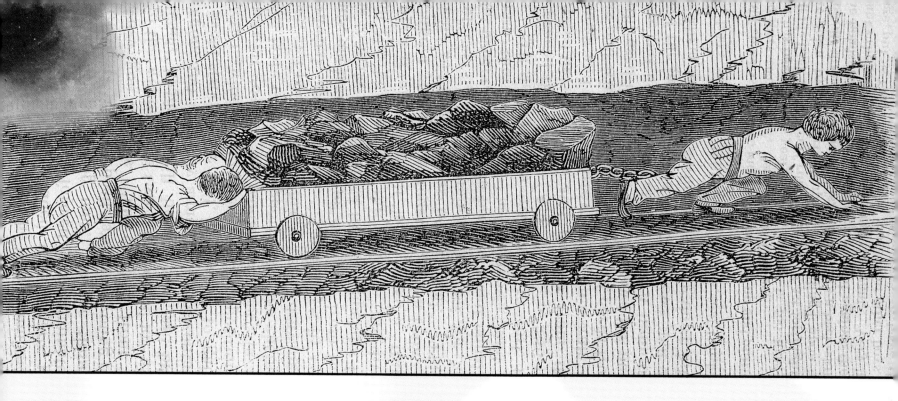

Chained at the waist, a boy scrambles up a mine shaft no more than 20 inches high pulling a wagonload of coal while the boys behind, known as "thrusters," push *(above)*. A slightly older boy, called a "getter," works on his back with a pick to free coal from the mine face *(below)*.

"The roof is very low; I have to bend my back and legs. . . . Has no liking for the work; father makes me like it."

Janet Cumming, 11 years old

Working in the Mills

Washable, cheaper to produce, and easier to weave and dye, cotton supplanted wool as Britain's chief commodity in the 18th century. By a system known as "putting out," cotton cloth was produced by farm families who spun, wove, and dyed cotton between chores. But in 1785 a steam engine was first used to power a spinning factory, and by 1840 three-quarters of all Britain's cotton was spun on steam-driven machines. An entire class of skilled hand spinners and weavers became nearly extinct.

In their stead, a new group of textile workers emerged who commonly spent 12 to 16 hours a day in the lint-filled mills, risking fingers and limbs in machines that featured ceaselessly spinning bobbins and speeding shuttles. Many of these workers were women, but children worked there as well. Youngsters were cheaper to employ and, nimble and small, were perfect for scurrying beneath the looms, which never stopped, to oil and clean them.

The mills punished employees for infractions such as lateness, swearing, and horseplay with dismissals, fines, and corporal punishment, but not all mill owners were so harsh. Textile magnate and social reformer Robert Owen—who operated a mill at New Lanark, Scotland—housed, fed, and educated his workers and even exposed them to such refinements as ballroom dancing. Other reformers, notably Richard Oastler, campaigned rigorously against the use of children in the mills. Restrictions began in 1802, and by midcentury a series of Factory Acts limited, but did not abolish, child labor.

Nineteenth-century illustrations reveal two extremes of thought about millwork. In the idealized portrait at right, neatly dressed women and girls work at carding machines in a spacious setting. At far right, a top-hatted mill owner oversees his workers, oblivious to the beating one is about to receive.

"It is by iron fingers, teeth, and wheels . . . that the cotton is opened, cleaned, spread, carded, drawn, roved, spun, wound, warped, dressed, and woven."

Workers, Unite!

Fearful of the violence that had rampaged through Revolutionary France, Parliament came down hard on the organizing of industrial workers. Laws passed in 1799 and 1800 made it illegal for workers to join unions, though some did in secret under the guise of benevolent societies. The laws were repealed in 1824, and membership in trade unions skyrocketed. The card above, issued in 1833, shows its bearer to be a member of the West of Scotland Power Loom Female Weavers Society.

Adjusting to City Life

Since workers needed to be housed near their jobs, the population of many small towns that were near mills and coal fields increased by four and five times during the first half of the 19th century. Families crowded into existing tenements, which were subdivided into what were called "rookeries" because they resembled little more than roosts for birds.

With no urban planning or building codes, unscrupulous speculators quickly erected block after block of row-style houses, often separated by no more than a thickness of half a brick and lacking even the most primitive sanitary facilities. Twenty or more families might share a single privy, with one standpipe serving as the water source for an entire neighborhood. Until 1825 windows were taxed, compounding the problem of dark and airless housing. The close quarters were breeding grounds for diseases such as typhoid and cholera, though many lives were also lost to malnutrition and tuberculosis.

In the textile center of Leeds, infant mortality rates, industrial accidents, and disease combined to end an average resident's life at 19. In Liverpool, the normal life expectancy did not exceed 15. Since most women worked, the problem of child care was usually handled by an older woman enlisted to watch children too young to work themselves. Fussy babies were commonly sedated with opium preparations formulated just for them.

Since farm laborers often were not paid at all, a shilling a day, about 12 1/2 cents, was considered a good wage for the new industrial worker. Wages were usually paid out on Saturdays, just in time to be spent in the beer shops and gin palaces by workers seeking quick relief from their grim circumstances. In London there was no minimum age for drinking and, until 1839, no limit on operating hours for pubs.

"I have earned no money today; but pray, sir, don't tell anybody of it. I could never bear the thought of going to the workhouse."
—A 60-year-old woman

Seeking to improve the workers' plight, reformers sensationalized their living conditions, as in these illustrations of a London tenement house strung with laundry and of half-starved children scavenging for food in a pig trough.

Although workhouses, which offered shelter, food, and employment to the destitute, were an improvement over earlier poor law legislation, conditions were kept spartan to discourage long stays. In London's Field Lane Refuge, workers slept in coffinlike beds.

Traveling by Rail

No other single invention of the age offered more excitement and hope for the future than did the steam locomotive *(below)*. Introduced in 1814 by engineer George Stephenson, the locomotive was designed to transport coal from the mines to the mills. Eleven years later, Stephenson offered the first rail passenger service, and a passion for trains was ignited all across Britain.

Houses and shops by the hundreds were knocked down to make way for the new track, laid by hardworking, hard-drinking, mostly Irish laborers known as "navvies," short for navigators. In 1838, Britain had only 500 miles of track. Ten years later the navvies had laid an incredible 5,000 miles of rails and ties. Now newspapers, mail, and fresh produce from the farms reached urban dwellers in large quantities and at record-breaking speed.

And nothing drew bigger crowds than the locomotives on display at the Great Exhibition of 1851, held as a testament to Britain's industrial might. Six million visitors jammed the Crystal Palace, an iron and glass exhibition hall covering 19 acres in London's Hyde Park, to marvel at the world's technical and industrial achievements, including a huge array of steam-powered machines: farm tools, boilers, cranes, looms, and the revered locomotives.

> ## "We are capable of doing anything."
> **Queen Victoria, 1851**

The machinery hall in the British section of the Great Exhibition of 1851, depicted in the lithograph at right, offered tangible proof of Britain's technological and industrial superiority.

GLOSSARY

Absolute monarchy: a monarchy in which the powers of the king are not limited by laws or a constitution.

Advent: the religious season before Christmas, which includes the four previous Sundays.

Allemande: a 17th- and 18th-century dance and its accompanying music.

Ancien régime: literally, "old regime." The political and social system in France before the French Revolution of 1789.

Annus mirabilis: literally, "wonderful year." Used to describe the year-long period from 1797 to 1798 when Romantic writers William Wordsworth and Samuel Taylor Coleridge lived near each other in Somerset and produced their book of poetry entitled *Lyrical Ballads.*

Anti-Semite: one who discriminates against or is prejudiced or hostile toward Jews.

Arrondissement: an administrative district in a large French city.

Ballad: a simple narrative poem, often set to music.

Baroque: a highly ornate, extravagant style of the 17th and 18th centuries.

Bastille: an old fortress in Paris that had come to symbolize the despotism of the ancien régime. On July 14, 1789, an angry mob stormed the Bastille after the governor refused to surrender arms and munitions stored there. The fall of the Bastille heralded the beginning of the French Revolution.

Biedermeier: period in Germany from 1815 to 1848 characterized by a simple and charming style of painting, furniture, poetry, and music. Biedermeier style was partly a reaction to the political upheavals of the preceding decades and to the wild emotions of the Romantics. The Biedermeier era fostered newfound pride in all things German and a move toward nationalism.

Blank verse: unrhymed verse.

Bonapartists: adherents of the Bonapartes or their policies.

Bourbon: name of the royal family that ruled in France from 1589 to 1792.

Bourbon Restoration: One of the Bourbons, Louis XVIII, returned the family to the throne in 1814 after the fall of Napoleon. The Restoration was responsible for considerable economic recovery in France and for the improvement of France's prestige abroad. The Bourbon Restoration ended in 1830 with a coup d'état that established a constitutional monarchy.

Bourgeoisie: the French middle class.

Cantata: a choral composition consisting of a narrative with vocal solos, often accompanied by a chorus and an orchestra.

Capitalism: an economic system in which the making and distribution of goods depends on privately invested money and profit-making.

Catechism: a summary of the principles of religious doctrine, usually in a question-and-answer format.

Chamber music: music suited for performance by a few instruments in a room or small concert hall.

Chloroform: a colorless, volatile, pungent liquid, formerly used as a general anesthetic.

Chokedamp: in mines, a noxious atmosphere low in oxygen and high in carbon dioxide.

Citizen king: Louis-Philippe, who ruled France from 1830 to 1848. He deserted the French Revolution in 1793 and lived in exile for 20 years, returning to France after the Bourbon Restoration. His reign, called the July monarchy, was supported by the upper middle class and the press; his beliefs were in opposition to those held by former kings Louis XVIII and Charles X.

Civil marriage: a marriage performed by a government official instead of a member of the clergy.

Comédie Française: the national theater of France.

Communism: a system of social organization based on the holding of all property in common, with actual ownership belonging to the community as a whole or to the state.

Concerto: a musical composition for one instrument or for one or more instruments accompanied by an orchestra.

Confederation of the Rhine: a league of German states formed by Napoleon in 1806 after he defeated the Austrians at Austerlitz. Nearly every German state, except Austria and Prussia, joined. The confederation collapsed after Napoleon's retreat from Russia in 1812.

Congress of Vienna: an international conference in 1814-1815, following the banishment of Napoleon to Elba and the demise of his empire. The purpose of the conference, which was attended by most of Europe's rulers, was to reestablish territorial boundaries and to restore the crowned heads of Europe to their thrones.

Conscript: a person recruited by the state, usually for military service.

Constitution: a body of principles by which a state is governed.

Constitutional monarchy: a monarchy in which the king is subject to laws set forth in a constitution.

Consulate: the government in France from 1799 to 1804 that took the place of the Directory. Napoleon Bonaparte was appointed one of three consuls and, in practice, dominated the government.

Cortege: a procession, usually for a funeral.

Counterrevolutionary: a person who opposes a revolution or revolutionary government.

Coup d'état: a sudden and decisive change of government, usually through use of force.

Courtesan: a prostitute with wealthy clients; mistress of a nobleman.

Courtier: a person in attendance at a royal court.

Cricket: an English sport played on a grass field with two teams of 11 players taking turns bowling toward a wicket defended by a batting player of the other team.

Curate: a clergyman who assists a parish priest or vicar.

Daguerreotype: a photographic process invented in 1839 by Frenchman Louis Daguerre that produced a permanent image on a silver sheet sensitized with iodine and exposed to mercury vapor.

Declaration of the Rights of Man and of the Citizen: a document drafted and passed by France's National Assembly in 1789, which asserted men's rights to liberty, private property, freedom from oppression, equality before the law, and freedom of expression, of the press, and of religion. The document also stated that sovereignty resided in the state and that the monarch was to be subordinate to the law. The declaration became the preamble to France's Constitution of 1791.

Directory: a regime lasting from 1795 to 1799, consisting of a bicameral legislative body and a five-man executive branch that held power in France in accordance with the nation's constitution. Public dissatisfaction with the Directory grew, and it was overthrown on November 9, 1799, and replaced with the Consulate. Three consuls were named, including Napoleon Bonaparte.

Duchy: the territory ruled by a duke or duchess.

Elector: a German prince entitled to take part in the election of the Holy Roman emperor.

Émigré: a French refugee, usually a royalist, who sought residence in another country during the French Revolution.

Empire style: a style of clothing and furnishings associated with France's First Empire. The style was characterized by the use of Classical, Egyptian, or military motifs.

Enlightenment: an intellectual movement of the 17th and 18th centuries. Sometimes called the Age of Reason, its focus was on a rational understanding of the natural world and man's role in it. At its heart was a conflict between religion and the desire to know and understand the world on the basis of experimentation and physical evidence.

Estates-General: the national representative body formed in 1302 consisting of delegates from

France's three social classes: the clergy and the nobles, who made up the First and Second Estates, and the common people, who comprised the Third Estate.

Factory Acts: a series of laws enacted during the Industrial Revolution in England that tried to curb the exploitation of workers and limited, but did not abolish, child labor.

Feudal system: the social system in medieval Europe in which a lord allowed vassals to occupy his lands in exchange for allegiance and service.

Firedamp: a combustible gas found in coal mines which consists mainly of methane and which can be explosive when mixed with air.

Foxglove: any plant belonging to the genus *Digitalis,* having spikes of purple or white bell-shaped flowers; the source of medicinal digitalis, used in the treatment of congestive heart failure.

Franc: the chief monetary unit of France.

Francophobe: a person who fears or dislikes France or the French.

German Confederation: a loose political association of German states formed in 1815 by the Congress of Vienna.

Girondist: a member of a political group formed during the French Revolution made up of moderate republicans. Its leaders were at odds with the radical Jacobins. The group fell apart in May 1793 when more than two dozen of its members were arrested and executed.

Gobelins tapestry workshop: a state-controlled tapestry manufacturing facility in Paris. Founded as a dyeworks in the mid-15th century by Jean Gobelin.

Gout: a disease that painfully inflames the joints, mainly in the hands and feet and particularly the big toe; caused by excessive uric acid in the blood.

Grande Armée: the army of Emperor Napoleon I. It fought numerous battles to expand Napoleon's empire and power.

Grand Chamberlain: an official who manages the household of a sovereign or a member of the nobility.

Grand tour: a cultural tour of western Europe for educational purposes, usually taken by the sons of Britain's wealthy families.

Great Exhibition of 1851: an exposition held as a testament to Britain's industrial might. Six million visitors attended, viewing technical and industrial achievements from all over the world, including an array of steam-powered machines.

Grenadier: the first regiment of the royal household infantry; a soldier armed with grenades.

Gueridon: a style of table popular during the Empire era featuring a small top set on a pedestal; it was sometimes folded for storage.

Guillotine: a beheading device with a heavy blade that drops between two posts, used for executions.

Haberdasher: a merchant who sells men's clothing and accessories.

Habsburg: a royal family of Europe that provided sovereigns for the thrones of the Holy Roman Empire, Austria, Spain, and others.

Hieroglyphics: a pictographic script used by the ancient Egyptians.

Hofburg: a vast imperial residential compound in Vienna, built by the Habsburgs; the complex grew with the empire, the earliest section dating from the 13th century and the last building being completed in 1913.

Holy Roman Empire: a loosely federated, primarily Germanic, central European political entity, which included an amalgam of affiliated duchies, counties, cities, and principalities.

Honorarium: a voluntary payment for professional services rendered without a set fee.

Hôtel de Ville: the city hall in Paris.

Impressionism: a style of painting that uses short brushstrokes and bright colors to convey the effect of light on objects.

Industrial Revolution: a period of economic and social reorganization from the middle of the 18th century to the middle of the 19th century resulting from industry's replacement of hand tools with steam-powered machines.

Jacobins: a political wing formed during the French Revolution that consisted mainly of bourgeois members of the Third Estate who sought to limit the powers of the king. The term soon became synonymous with radical activism.

July monarchy: name attached to the reign of "citizen king" Louis-Philippe; so called because his rule began after the overthrow of Charles X in July 1830.

Kapellmeister: choir master or musical director.

Karlsbad Decrees: decrees issued by the German Confederation in 1819 that increased censorship and outlawed groups that wanted the confederation abolished and a true national government established.

Lancet: a small, broad surgical knife with two cutting edges and a sharp point.

Laudanum: a tincture made with opium, used at one time for medicinal purposes.

Lent: the annual religious season of fasting and penitence in preparation for Easter, lasting for 40 weekdays between Ash Wednesday and Easter Sunday.

Liberal: a person who advocated curtailing governmental power and protecting the rights of individual citizens.

Libertine: a freethinker regarding religion.

Lied (pl. lieder): a poetic song in which the vocal line and the musical accompaniment are of equal musical significance. The lied style was articulated by 19th-century German composers such as Schubert and Brahms.

Marquis: a nobleman who ranks below a duke and above a count.

Méridienne: a short sofa of the Empire period with a sloping back connected to arms of unequal height; a chaise longue.

Merveilleuses: literally, "the marvelous ones." Members of France's middle class who became weary of revolution and busied themselves making money and merriment.

Metallurgy: the science of the production, purification, and properties of metals.

Monarchy: a government headed by a single person whose right to rule is usually hereditary.

Musée Napoleon: Napoleon Bonaparte's museum in Paris (now the Louvre); used to display artwork from around the world, much of which was confiscated during Napoleon's military campaigns.

Napoleonic Code: the civil code of France, passed in 1804; a cornerstone of Napoleon's administration.

National Assembly: a legislative body formed by some members of the Estates-General, it produced France's first constitution.

National workshops: workshops that provided government-financed work in France to the unemployed.

Neoclassicism: a revival of the Classical style in art, literature, music, architecture, and so on.

Nitrous oxide: a colorless, sweet-smelling, non-flammable gas used as an anesthetic; also called laughing gas.

Objet d'art: an object of some artistic value.

Old Master: a great artist of another era, particularly of the 13th to 17th centuries in Europe.

Opium: an addictive drug extracted from the opium poppy; used as an analgesic and a narcotic.

Oratorio: a dramatic musical composition, often based on a sacred theme. It is performed with instrumentation and singing (typically a chorus, an orchestra, and soloists) but without costumes, scenery, or other effects.

Ottoman Empire: a vast state founded in the 13th century by Turkish tribes in Anatolia and ruled by the descendants of Osman I until its dissolution in 1918. The empire encompassed parts of southeastern Europe, western Asia, and northern Africa.

Overture: an orchestral piece at the beginning of an opera or oratorio.

Parliament: England's legislative body, consisting of the House of Lords and the House of Commons.

Pianoforte: a piano.

Pithead: the area around a mine shaft's entrance.

Pogrom: an organized massacre, especially of Jews.

Polonaise: a dance of Polish origin and the music that accompanies it.

Polyglot: multilingual.

Prater: large park located on the Danube in Vienna.

Press: a machine that applies pressure in order to compress, flatten, shape, extract, or punch shapes; or newspapers and periodicals and the people who produce them.

Principality: a state ruled by a prince.

Privateer: an armed, privately owned ship authorized by a government during wartime to prey upon and capture or sink the ships of the enemy or, during peacetime, those of pirates.

Protestant: follower of any of the western Christian religions that are separate from the Roman Catholic Church.

Rationalism: a belief in reason as life's guiding principle.

Reign of Terror: period (1793-1794) during the French Revolution in which thousands of people deemed enemies of the state were executed.

Relay post: a way station for stagecoach travelers in the French countryside, positioned about every 10 miles so that horse teams could be fed and watered or replaced.

Renaissance: the great revival of Classical art, literature, and learning in 14th- to 16th-century Europe.

Republic: a government in which power is held by the people entitled to vote and exercised by the representatives they have chosen.

Romanticism: a literary and artistic movement of the 18th and 19th centuries resulting, in part, from the libertarian and egalitarian ideals of the French Revolution. Romantics rejected the Enlightenment and its emphasis on reason and embraced intuition, feeling, inspiration, and individualism.

Rosetta stone: a carved stone that bears parallel inscriptions in Greek and Egyptian characters, providing a key to deciphering Egyptian hieroglyphics. Discovered in Egypt in 1799 by members of Napoleon's archaeological team.

Royalist: one who supports a monarchy, especially in times of revolution.

Ruhe und Ordnung: literally, "tranquillity and order." A slogan used to describe the new Europe after Napoleon's fall.

Salon: a regular, informal gathering of eminent people usually hosted by a woman. Salons were a central feature of aristocratic and intellectual life in the 17th and 18th centuries.

Schubertiaden: gatherings held to listen to the music of Franz Schubert.

Scurvy: a disease caused by a vitamin C deficiency.

Smallpox: an acute, contagious disease caused by a virus and characterized by pustular skin eruptions. A smallpox vaccine was developed in 1796 by English physician Edward Jenner.

Socialism: a political and economic system of collective government that vests ownership in production and capital in the community as a whole.

Sonata: a musical composition for one or two instruments.

Spanish Riding School: famed facility in Vienna where Lippizaner horses are trained to perform movements of 17th-century dressage.

Steam engine: an engine that uses the expansive properties of steam to generate power.

Stethoscope: a medical instrument created in 1816 by René Laënnec that is used to listen to the action of the heart and lungs.

String quartet: a musical composition for four string instruments, typically two violins, a viola, and a cello.

Sturm und Drang: literally, "storm and stress." A German literary movement that advocated intense emotionalism.

Sublime: inspiring awe and veneration or a sense of grandeur or power.

Symphony: an elaborate musical composition of three or four movements, usually written for a full orchestra.

Théâtre de l'Ambigu-Comique: one of Paris's most popular playhouses.

Tocsin: a warning bell or the ringing of it.

Tuileries: a former royal palace in Paris.

Ultraroyalist: a French citizen who desired total restoration of the monarchy.

Violoncello: the formal name for a cello.

Volk: a German word meaning "people."

Wallpaper: an inexpensive wallcovering first used in Europe in the 16th and 17th centuries in lieu of costly hangings. French wallpaper of the best quality was produced by Jean-Baptiste Réveillon in the early 19th century.

Waltz: a graceful ballroom dance performed by couples and the music for this dance, extremely popular in the 19th century.

Workhouse: a place where the poor received lodging in return for work done.

PRONUNCIATION GUIDE

Académie des Sciences ah-kah-day-MEE day see-AHNS

Ajaccio ah-YAH-choh

Amati ah-MAH-tee

Amiens ah-mee-YEHN

Antoine-Jean Gros ahn-TWAHN-zhahn groh

Arnault ahr-NOH

Arnstein AHRN-shtine

Auguste oh-GOOST

Aurore Dudevant oh-ROHR DOO-duh-vahn

Autun oh-TUHN

Baden BAHD-ehn

Beauharnais boh-ahr-NAY

Beaux Arts bohz ahr

Biedermeier BEE-duhr-meye-uhr

Bordeaux bohr-DOH

Bourbon BOOR-bohn

Breuning BROY-nihng

Brunsvik BROONS-vihk

Calais kah-LAY

Chalais shah-LAY

Chopin shoh-pan

Cimarosa chee-mah-ROH-zuh

Comédie Française koh-may-DEE frahn-SEHZ

Comte kohnt

Concordat kohn-kohr-DAH

Coppet koh-PAY

Curchod koor-SHOH

Daguerre dah-GAYR

Dauphiné doh-fee-NAY

David dah-VEED

Delphine dehl-FEEN

Domanovecz DOH-mah-noh-vehtch

Dumas doo-MAH

Eisenstadt EYE-zen-shtaht

Erdödy ehr-DOH-dee

Esterházy EHS-tehr-hah-zee

Eugène Delacroix yoo-ZHEHN dehl-ah-KRWAH

Faust fowst

Frankfurt am Main FRAHNK-foort ahm mine

Friedrich FREE-drihk

Georges Danton zhorzh dahn-tohn

Géricault zhay-ree-koh
Germaine de Staël zhehr-man duh stahl
Girondins zhee-rohn-DAN
Giulietta Guicciardi jool-YEHT-tuh gweet-CHAHR-dee
Glacis glah-SEE
Gluck glook
Gobelins goh-beh-LAN
Goethe GEH-teh
Göttingen GEH-tihng-ehn
Graben GRAH-behn
Guarneri gwahr-NYEHR-ee
Gueridons gehr-eh-DOHN
Guillotine GEE-oh-teen
Haydn HIDE-ehn
Heiligenstadt HEYE-lih-gen-shtaht
Hernani hehr-NAH-nee
Hesse-Kassel HEHS-suh-KAH-suhl
Honoré de Balzac ohn-oh-RAY duh bahl-ZAHK
Hôtel de Ville oh-TEL duh veel
Jacobins zhah-ko-BAN
Jahn yahn
Jardins des Plantes zhahr-DAN day plahnt
Josephstradt YOH-zef-shtraht
Jules Sandeau zhool sahn-DOH
Jullien zhool-YEHN
Kappellmeister kah-PEHL-meye-stehr
Lamartine lah-mahr-TEEN

Les Misérables lay mee-zehr-AHB-leh
Les Trois Mousquetaires lay trwah moo-skuh-TAYR
Letizia leh-TEET-see-uh
Lichnowsky lihk-NAHF-skee
Lobkowitz LOHB-koh-vits
Louis-Philippe lwee-fee-LEEP
Louis XVI lwee sez
Louveciennes loo-veh-SEE-ehn
Louvre LOOV-reh
Lyon lyohn
Maria Ludovica mah-REE-ah loo-doh-VEE-kah
Marseilles mahr-SAY
Méridienne meh-ree-DEE-EHN
Merveilleuses mehr-veh-YEUHZ
Metternich MEHT-tuhr-neehk
Mirabeau mee-rah-BOH
Montmartre mohn-MAHRT-ruh
Musset myoo-SAY
Objets d'art ohb-zhay dahr
Orléans ohr-lay-AHN
Percier pehr-syay
Pinel pee-NEHL
Place du Châtelet plahss doo shah-tuh-LAY
Prater PRAH-tuhr
Provence proh-VAHNS
Razumovsky rah-tsoo-MOHF-skee
Recamier ray-kah-MYAY

Réveillon reh-vay-YOHN
Ries rees
Robespierre ROH-behs-pyehr
Rue St. Denis roo SAN duh-NEE
Ruhe und Ordnung ROO-eh oond OHRD-noong
Salieri sahl-YAYR-ee
Savigny SAH-vihn-yee
Schlegel SHLAY-guhl
Schubertiaden shoo-behr-TEE-AH-dehn
Schwind shvihnt
Scribe skreeb
Seine sehn
Talleyrand tahl-leh-rahn
Théâtre de l'Ambigu Comique tay-AHT-reh duh LAHM-bee-gyoo koh-MEEK
Tocqueville tohk-VEEL
Toulon too-LOHN
Trautmansdorff TROUT-mahns-dohrf
Tuileries twee-luh-REE
Vallon vuhl-LOHN
Versailles vehr-SEYE
Vicomte vee-kohnt
Viehmann FEE-mahn
Vigée-Lebrun vee-zhay-luh-bruhn
Waldstein VAHLD-shtine
Wild veeld
Württemberg VEWR-tehm-behrg

ACKNOWLEDGMENTS AND PICTURE CREDITS

ACKNOWLEDGMENTS

The editors wish to thank the following individuals and institutions for their valuable assistance in the preparation of this volume:
Udo Baron von Brentano, Oestrich-Winkel im Rheingau; Jens Dufner, Beethoven-Haus Bonn, Bonn; Mary Ison and Staff, Library of Congress, Washington, D.C.; Heidrun Klein, Bildarchiv Preussischer Kulturbesitz, Berlin; William Meredith, Ph.D., San Jose State University, San Jose, Calif.; Daniela Müller, Städtische Galerie im Lenbachhaus, Munich; Petra Rau, Freies Deutsches Hochstift-Frankfurter Goethe Museum, Frankfurt am Main; Helmut Selzer, Historisches Museum der Stadt Wien, Vienna; George Syamken, Hamburger Kunsthalle, Hamburg.

PICTURE CREDITS

The sources for the illustrations that appear in this volume are listed below. Credits from left to right are separated by semicolons, from top to bottom by dashes.

Cover: Photo RMN, Paris.

1-5: Roy Miles, Esq./The Bridgeman Art Library, London. 6, 7: Waltraud Klammet/Ohlstadt. 8-11: Border adapted from a photo from Städtische Galerie im Lenbachhaus, Munich. Detail from *Dornröschen* by E. N. Neureuther. 12, 13: Map by John Drummond, © Time Life Inc.; map compass art by John Drummond, © Time Life Inc., adapted from a photo from Photo Josse, Paris. 14, 15: Lauros-Giraudon, Paris; Collection du Mobilier national, cliché du Mobilier national/Ph. Sébert. 17: City of Bristol Museum and Art Gallery, UK/The Bridgeman Art Library, London. 18: Lauros-Giraudon, Paris. 19: Courtesy of the National Portrait Gallery, London. 20, 21: Mary Evans Picture Library, London. 23: Photo RMN, Paris-Gérard Blot/Louvre, Paris; Bibliothèque nationale de France, Paris. 24-27: Background EyeWire, Inc.; border adapted from a photo from Bibliothèque nationale de France, Paris. 24, 25: Louvre, Paris/The

Bridgeman Art Library, London. 26, 27: Photo RMN, Paris-Gérard Blot; Christie's Images, London/The Bridgeman Art Library, London—Partridge Fine Arts, London/The Bridgeman Art Library, London. 28: Musée du Chateau, Versailles/Photo Josse, Paris. 30: Photo RMN, Paris-Arnaudet. 31: Private Collection/The Bridgeman Art Library, London. 32-35: Giraudon, Paris. 36: Archiv für Kunst und Geschichte (AKG), Berlin/Louvre, Paris, photo by Erich Lessing, Vienna. 39: Louvre, Paris/Photo Josse, Paris. 40: Gianni Dagli Orti, Paris. 42: Musée du Romantisme, Paris/Photo Josse, Paris. 44, 45: Photo RMN, Paris. 46, 47: Collection de la Société Française de Photographie. 48: Giraudon, Paris. 50, 51: Musée de la Ville de Paris, Musée du Petit-Palais/The Bridgeman Art Library, London. 52-60: Background EyeWire, Inc.; border adapted from a photo from Musée des Tissus de Lyon/Studio Basset. 52, 53: Musée des Tissus de Lyon/Studio Basset; Photo RMN, Paris. 54, 55: Wallace Collection, Lon-

BIBLIOGRAPHY

BOOKS

Abrantès, Laure Junot, duchesse d'. *At the Court of Napoleon.* N.Y.: Doubleday, 1989.

The Age of Napoleon. N.Y.: Metropolitan Museum of Art, 1989.

Alsop, Susan Mary. *The Congress Dances.* N.Y.: Harper & Row, 1984.

Altham, H. S. *A History of Cricket,* Vol. 1. London: George Allen & Unwin, 1962.

Anchor, Robert. *Germany Confronts Modernization.* Lexington, Mass.: D. C. Heath and Co., 1972.

Andrews, Wayne. *Germaine.* N.Y.: Atheneum, 1963.

Aries, Philippe. *Centuries of Childhood.* N.Y.: Vintage Books, 1962.

The Art of the July Monarchy: France 1830 to 1848.

Columbia: University of Missouri Press, 1990.

Artz, Frederick B. *France under the Bourbon Restoration, 1814-1830.* N.Y.: Russell & Russell, 1963.

Autexier, Philippe. *Beethoven.* Trans. by Carey Lovelace. London: Thames and Hudson, 1992.

Baillio, Joseph. *Elisabeth Louise Vigée Le Brun.* Fort Worth, Tex.: Kimbell Art Museum, 1982.

Barraclough, G. *The Origins of Modern Germany.* N.Y.: W. W. Norton & Co., 1984.

Bate, Walter Jackson. *Coleridge.* N.Y.: Macmillan, 1968.

Bernard, J. F. *Talleyrand: A Biography.* N.Y.: G. P. Putnam's Sons, 1973.

Black, Jeremy, and Roy Porter, eds. *The Penguin Dictionary of Eighteenth-Century History.* N.Y.: Penguin, 1994.

Blyth, Henry. *Caro, the Fatal Passion: The Life of Lady*

Caroline Lamb. N.Y.: Coward, McCann & Geoghegan, 1972.

Boyle, Nicholas. *Goethe: The Poet and the Age,* Vol. 1. Oxford: Clarendon Press, 1991.

Briggs, Asa. *Everyday Life through the Ages.* London: Reader's Digest, 1992.

Brose, Eric Dorn. *German History, 1789-1871.* Providence, R.I.: Berghahn Books, 1997.

Cairns, Trevor. *Power for the People.* Minneapolis: Lerner, 1980.

Cambridge Historical Encyclopedia of Great Britain and Ireland. Cambridge: Cambridge University Press, 1985.

The Cambridge Illustrated History of Medicine. Ed. by Roy Porter. Cambridge: Cambridge University Press, 1996.

Cameron, Kenneth Neill, ed. *Romantic Rebels.* Cambridge, Mass.: Harvard University Press, 1973.

Carr, Philip. *Days with the French Romantics in the Paris of 1830.* London: Methuen & Co., 1932.

Carroll, Bob. *The Importance of Napoleon Bonaparte.* San Diego, Calif.: Lucent Books, 1994.

Cate, Curtis. *George Sand: A Biography.* Boston: Houghton Mifflin, 1975.

Charlton, D. G., ed. *The French Romantics,* Vol. 1. Cambridge: Cambridge University Press, 1984.

The Complete Grimm's Fairy Tales. Trans. by Margaret Hunt. N.Y.: Pantheon Books, 1972.

Croft-Cooke, Rupert, and Peter Cotes. *Circus: A World History.* N.Y.: Macmillan, 1976.

Crowther, M. A. *The Workhouse System, 1834-1929.* Athens: University of Georgia Press, 1982.

Cultural Interactions in the Romantic Age: Critical Essays in Comparative Literature. Ed. by Gregory Maertz. Albany: State University of New York Press, 1998.

Delderfield, R. F. *Napoleon in Love.* N.Y.: Simon and Schuster, 1959.

Dickenson, Donna. *George Sand: A Brave Man—the Most Womanly Woman.* Oxford: Berg, 1988.

Drabble, Margaret. *Wordsworth.* N.Y.: Arco, 1969.

Dupeux, Georges. *French Society: 1789-1970.* Trans. by Peter Wait. London: Methuen & Co., 1972.

Durant, Will, and Ariel Durant. *The Age of Napoleon: A History of European Civilization from 1789 to 1815,* Vol. 11 of *The Story of Civilization.* N.Y.: MJF Books, 1975.

Edwards, Samuel. *George Sand: A Biography of the First Modern, Liberated Woman.* N.Y.: David McKay, 1972.

Einstein, Alfred. *Music in the Romantic Era.* N.Y.: W. W. Norton & Co., 1947.

Eisler, Benita. *Byron: Child of Passion, Fool of Fame.* N.Y.: Alfred A. Knopf, 1999.

Encyclopedia of Romanticism: Culture in Britain, 1780s-1830s. Ed. by Laura Dabundo. N.Y.: Garland Publishing, 1992.

Erickson, Carolly. *Our Tempestuous Day.* N.Y.: William Morrow and Co., 1986.

Events that Changed the World in the Nineteenth Century. Ed. by Frank W. Thackeray and John E. Findling. Westport, Conn.: Greenwood Press, 1996.

Fairley, John. *Racing in Art.* N.Y.: Rizzoli, 1990.

Ford, John. *Prizefighting: The Age of Regency Boximania.* N.Y.: Great Albion Books, 1971.

Fortescue, William. *Alphonse de Lamartine.* London: Croom Holm, 1983.

The French Revolution of 1789 and Its Impact. Ed. by Gail M. Schwab and John R. Jeanneney. Westport, Conn.: Greenwood Press, 1995.

Freytag, Gustav. *Pictures of German Life,* Vol. 2. London: Chapman and Hall, 1863.

Fruman, Norman. *Coleridge, the Damaged Archangel.* N.Y.: George Braziller, 1971.

Garland, Henry, and Mary Garland. *The Oxford Companion to German Literature.* Oxford: Oxford University Press, 1986.

Garraty, John A., and Peter Gay. *The Columbia History of the World.* N.Y.: Harper & Row, 1972.

Germaine de Staël. Ed. by Madelyn Gutwirth, Avriel Goldberger, and Karyna Szmurlo. New Brunswick, N.J.: Rutgers University Press, 1991.

Gernsheim, Helmut:
    A Concise History of Photography. N.Y.: Dover, 1986.
    Creative Photography: Aesthetic Trends, 1839-1960. N.Y.: Dover Publications, 1962.

Goodden, Angelica. *The Sweetness of Life: A Biography of Elisabeth Louise Vigée Le Brun.* London: Andre Deutsch, 1997.

Gonzalez-Palacios, Alvar. *The French Empire Style.* Trans. by Raymond Rudorff. London: Hamlyn, 1970.

Gottlieb, Beatrice. *The Family in the Western World from the Black Death to the Industrial Age.* N.Y.: Oxford University Press, 1993.

Grandjean, Serge. *Empire Furniture: 1800-1825.* N.Y.: Taplinger, 1966.

Grosskurth, Phyllis. *Byron: The Flawed Angel.* Boston: Houghton Mifflin, 1997.

Halévy, Elie. *England in 1815,* Vol. 1. Trans. by E. I. Watkin and D. A. Barker. London: Ernest Benn, 1968.

Halliday, F. E. *Wordsworth and His World.* N.Y.: Viking Press, 1970.

Hart, Roger. *English Life in the Nineteenth Century.* N.Y.: G. P. Putnam's Sons, 1971.

Hartt, Frederick. *Art: A History of Painting, Sculpture, and Architecture.* N.Y.: Harry N. Abrams, 1976.

Hayter, Alethea. *Opium and the Romantic Imagination.* Berkeley: University of California Press, 1968.

Henderson, Harry. *The Age of Napoleon* (World History series). San Diego, Calif.: Lucent Books, 1999.

Herold, J. Christopher:
    The Horizon Book of the Age of Napoleon. N.Y.: Horizon, 1963.
    Mistress to an Age: A Life of Madame de Staël. Indianapolis: Bobbs-Merrill, 1958.

Herrmann, Luke. *Turner: Paintings, Watercolours, Prints & Drawings.* N.Y.: Da Capo, 1975.

Hibbert, Christopher. *The English: A Social History, 1066-1945.* N.Y.: W. W. Norton & Co., 1987.

Hill, John Spencer. *A Coleridge Companion.* London: Macmillan, 1983.

Hobsbawm, Eric. *The Age of Revolution: Europe, 1789-1848.* N.Y.: Barnes & Noble, 1962.

Hoffmeister, Gerhart, ed. *The French Revolution and the Age of Goethe.* Hildesheim, Germany: Georg Olms Verlag, 1989.

Holborn, Hajo. *A History of Modern Germany.* Princeton, N.J.: Princeton University Press, 1964.

Holmes, Richard:
    Coleridge: Darker Reflections, 1804-1834. N.Y.: Pantheon Books, 1998.
    Coleridge: Early Visions. N.Y.: Viking, 1989.

Honour, Hugh. *Romanticism.* N.Y.: Harper & Row, 1979.

Inglis, Brian. *Poverty and the Industrial Revolution.* London: Hodder and Stoughton, 1971.

Jacobs, Arthur. *A New Dictionary of Music.* Harmondsworth, Middlesex, England: Penguin Books, 1973.

Johnston, Kenneth R. *The Hidden Wordsworth.* N.Y.: W. W. Norton & Co., 1998.

Jonas, Gerald. *Dancing: The Pleasure, Power, and Art of Movement.* N.Y.: Harry N. Abrams, 1992.

Jones, Colin. *The Cambridge Illustrated History of France.* Cambridge: Cambridge University Press, 1994.

Jones, Peter. *The 1848 Revolutions.* Essex, U.K.: Longman, 1981.

Jones, Peter, ed. *The French Revolution: In Social and Political Perspective.* London: Arnold, 1996.

Johnson, Paul. *The Birth of the Modern: World Society, 1815-1830.* N.Y.: HarperCollins, 1991.

Jullien, Marc-Antoine. *From Jacobin to Liberal: Marc-Antoine Jullien.* Trans. and ed. by R. R. Palmer. Princeton, N.J.: Princeton University Press, 1993.

Kamenetsky, Christa. *The Brothers Grimm and Their Critics.* Athens: Ohio University Press, 1992.

Kennedy, Emmet. *A Cultural History of the French Revolution.* New Haven, Conn.: Yale University Press, 1989.

Kitchen, Martin. *The Cambridge Illustrated History of Germany.* Cambridge: Cambridge University Press, 1996.

Lacombe, Bernard de. *Talleyrand the Man.* Trans. by A. D'Alberti. London: Herbert & Daniel, 1911.

Lamartine, A. De. *History of the French Revolution of 1848,* Vol. 1. Trans. by Francis A. Durivage and William S. Chase. N.Y.: AMS Press, 1973 (reprint of 1854 edition).

Landon, H. C. Robbins, comp. and ed. *Beethoven: A Documentary Study.* Trans. by Richard Wadleigh and Eugene Hartzell. N.Y.: Macmillan, 1970.

Lawrence, Berta. *Coleridge and Wordsworth in Somerset.* Newton Abbot, Great Britain: David & Charles, 1970.

Lentz, Thierry. *Napoléon: Mon Ambition Était Grande.* Paris: Découvertes Gallimard, 1998.

Lewes, George Henry. *The Life of Goethe.* N.Y.: Frederick Ungar, 1965.

Lines, Clifford. *Companion to the Industrial Revolution.* N.Y.: Facts On File, 1990.

Loudon, Irvine, ed. *Western Medicine.* Oxford: Oxford University Press, 1997.

McGraw-Hill Encyclopedia of World Drama. N.Y.: McGraw-Hill, 1984.

Magraw, Roger. *France 1814-1915: The Bourgeois Century.* N.Y.: Oxford University Press, 1983.

Mahoney, John L. *William Wordsworth: A Poetic Life.* N.Y.: Fordham University Press, 1997.

Malcolmson, Robert W. *Popular Recreations in English Society.* Cambridge: Cambridge University Press, 1973.

Marek, George R. *Beethoven: A Biography of a Genius.* N.Y.: Funk & Wagnalls, 1969.

Marshall, Dorothy. *English People in the Eighteenth Century.* London: Longmans, Green and Co., 1956.

May, Arthur J. *Vienna in the Age of Franz Josef.* Norman: University of Oklahoma Press, 1966.

Menke, Frank G. *The Encyclopedia of Sports.* Garden City, N.J.: Doubleday & Co., 1977.

Michaelis-Jena, Ruth. *The Brothers Grimm.* N.Y.: Praeger, 1970.

Miles, Henry Downes. *Pugilistica: The History of British Boxing,* Vol. 1. Edinburgh: John Grant, 1906.

Mowat, R. B. *The Romantic Age: Europe in the Early Nineteenth Century.* London: George G. Harrap & Co., 1937.

Murray, Venetia. *An Elegant Madness: High Society in Regency England.* N.Y.: Viking, 1998.

Napoleon I. *Napoleon on Napoleon: An Autobiography of the Emperor.* Ed. by Somerset de Chair. London: Cassell, 1992.

O'Neill, Michael. *Percy Bysshe Shelley: A Literary Life.* N.Y.: St. Martin's Press, 1990.

Peppard, Murray B. *Paths through the Forest: A Biography of the Brothers Grimm.* N.Y.: Holt, Rinehart and Winston, 1971.

Pinkney, David H. *Decisive Years in France: 1840-1847.* Princeton, N.J.: Princeton University Press, 1986.

Pool, Daniel. *What Jane Austen Ate and Charles Dickens Knew.* N.Y.: Touchstone, 1993.

Porter, Roy. *English Society in the Eighteenth Century.* London: Penguin Books, 1990.

Price, Roger. *A Social History of Nineteenth-Century France.* N.Y.: Holmes & Meier, 1987.

Price, Roger, ed. *1848 in France.* Ithaca, N.Y.: Cornell University Press, 1975.

Priestley, J. B. *The Prince of Pleasure and His Regency 1811-20.* N.Y.: Harper & Row, 1969.

The Pulse of Enterprise: TimeFrame AD 1800-1850. Alexandria, Va.: Time-Life Books, 1990.

Quennell, Marjorie, and C. H. B. Quennell. *A History of Everyday Things in England: 1733 to 1851,* Vol. 3. London: B. T. Batsford, 1961.

Quennell, Peter. *Romantic England: Writing and Painting, 1717-1851.* N.Y.: Macmillan, 1970.

Raphael, Frederic. *Byron.* N.Y.: Thames and Hudson, 1982.

Reader, W. J. *Victorian England.* London: William Clowes and Sons, 1974.

Rebel Daughters. Ed. by Sara E. Melzer and Leslie W. Rabine. N.Y.: Oxford University Press, 1992.

Reid, Donald. *Paris Sewers and Sewermen.* Cambridge, Mass.: Harvard University Press, 1991.

Richards, C. J., trans. *The Life & Times of Napoleon.* Philadelphia: Curtis Publishing, 1966.

Robiquet, Jean:
Daily Life in France: Under Napoleon. Trans. by Violet M. Macdonald. N.Y.: Macmillan, 1963.
Daily Life in the French Revolution. Trans. by James Kirkup. N.Y.: Macmillan, 1965.

Rooke, Patrick. *The Industrial Revolution.* N.Y.: John Day, 1971.

Rousselot, Jean, ed. *Medicine in Art: A Cultural History.* N.Y.: McGraw-Hill Book Co., [1967].

Saint, Andrew, and Gillian Darley. *The Chronicles of London.* N.Y.: St. Martin's Press, 1994.

Schama, Simon. *Citizens: A Chronicle of the French Revolution.* N.Y.: Vintage Books, 1989.

Schmidt-Görg, Joseph, and Hans Schmidt, eds. *Ludwig van Beethoven.* Bonn: Beethoven-Archiv, 1974.

Schom, Alan. *Napoleon Bonaparte.* N.Y.: HarperCollins, 1997.

Schubert's Vienna. Ed. by Raymond Erickson. New Haven, Conn.: Yale University Press, 1997.

Seward, Desmond. *Napoleon's Family.* N.Y.: Viking, 1986.

Sheehan, James J. *German History, 1770-1866.* Oxford: Clarendon Press, 1989.

Siegfried, Susan L. *The Art of Louis-Léopold Boilly: Modern Life in Napoleonic France.* New Haven, Conn.: Yale University Press, 1995.

Solomon, Maynard. *Beethoven.* N.Y.: Schirmer Books, 1977.

Spark, Muriel. *Mary Shelley.* N.Y.: E. P. Dutton, 1987.

Spender, Harold. *Byron and Greece.* Folcroft, Pa.: Folcroft Library Editions, 1976 (reprint of 1924 edition).

Spiel, Hilde. *Fanny von Arnstein: A Daughter of the Enlightenment, 1758-1818.* Trans. by Christine Shuttleworth. N.Y.: Berg, 1991.

Stadelmann, Rudolph. *Social and Political History of the German 1848 Revolution.* Trans. by James G. Chastain. Athens: Ohio University Press, 1975.

Stearns, Peter N.:
1848: The Revolutionary Tide in Europe. N.Y.: W. W. Norton & Co., 1974.
European Society in Upheaval: Social History Since 1750. N.Y.: Macmillan, 1975.

Strong, Roy. *The Story of Britain.* N.Y.: Fromm International Publishing, 1996.

Talleyrand-Périgord, Charles Maurice de. *Memoirs of the Prince de Talleyrand,* Vol. 1. Trans. by Raphael Ledos de Beaufort. N.Y.: AMS, 1973 (reprint of 1891 edition).

Talmon, J. L. *Romanticism and Revolt: Europe, 1815-1848.* N.Y.: Harcourt, Brace & World, 1967.

Tatar, Maria. *The Hard Facts of the Grimms' Fairy Tales.* Princeton, N.J.: Princeton University Press, 1987.

Thompson, E. P. *The Romantics: England in a Revolutionary Age.* N.Y.: New Press, 1997.

Thompson, J. M. *Napoleon Bonaparte.* N.Y.: Barnes & Noble Books, 1996.

Tocqueville, Alexis de. *Recollections.* Trans. by George Lawrence, ed. by J. P. Mayer and A. P. Kerr. Garden City, N.Y.: Doubleday & Co., 1970.

Tomalin, Claire. *Shelley and His World.* N.Y.: Charles Scribner's Sons, 1980.

Toussaint, Hélène, et al. *French Painting.* Trans. by Christopher Sells and ed. by Virginia Spate. Sydney: Australian Gallery Directors Council, 1980.

Tovey, Donald Francis. *Essays in Musical Analysis, Vol. 1: Symphonies.* London: Oxford University Press, 1935.

Trevelyan, George Macaulay. *English Social History.* N.Y.: Longman, 1978.

Vamplew, Wray. *The Turf: A Social and Economic History of Horse Racing.* London: Allen Lane, 1976.

Van Abbe, Derek. *Goethe.* Lewisburg: Bucknell University Press, 1972.

Vaughan, William. *Romanticism and Art.* London: Thames and Hudson, 1994.

Vigée-Lebrun, Louise-Elisabeth. *The Memoirs of Elisabeth Vigée-Le Brun.* Trans. by Siân Evans. Bloomington: Indiana University Press, 1989.

Walvin, James. *A Child's World.* Harmondsworth, Middlesex, England: Penguin Books, 1982.

Ward, Adolphus William. *Germany: 1815-1890, Vol. 1.* Cambridge: Cambridge University Press, 1916.

Wetterau, Bruce. *The N.Y. Public Library Book of Chronologies.* N.Y.: Stonesong Press, 1990.

White, R. J. *Life in Regency England.* Ed. by Peter Quennell. London: B. T. Batsford, 1963.

Wilson-Smith, Timothy. *Napoleon and His Artists.* London: Constable, 1996.

Winegarten, Renee. *The Double Life of George Sand: Woman and Writer.* N.Y.: Basic Books, 1978.

Wollstonecraft, Mary. *A Vindication of the Rights of Woman.* Ed. by Miriam Brody Kramnick. N.Y.: Penguin Books, 1975.

Woloch, Isser. *The New Regime.* N.Y.: W. W. Norton & Co., 1994.

Wordsworth, Jonathan. *William Wordsworth and the Age of English Romanticism.* New Brunswick, N.J.: Rutgers University Press, 1987.

Writers for Children. Ed. by Jane M. Bingham. N.Y.: Charles Scribner's Sons, 1988.

Zanker von Meyer, Dorothee. *Ideal und Natur.* München: Bruckmann, 1993.

Zipes, Jack. *The Brothers Grimm.* N.Y.: Routledge, 1988.

PERIODICALS

Brier, Bob. "Napoleon in Egypt." *Archaeology,* May/June 1999.

The British Empire, 1972, no. 50.

OTHER SOURCES

Metropolitan Museum of Art. *The Arts under Napoleon.* Show catalogue, April 6-July 30, 1978. N.Y.: Metropolitan Museum of Art, 1978.

INDEX

Numerals in italics indicate an illustration of the subject mentioned.

Time-Life Books is a division of Time Life Inc.

TIME LIFE INC.

CHAIRMAN AND CHIEF EXECUTIVE OFFICER:
Jim Nelson
PRESIDENT AND CHIEF OPERATING OFFICER:
Steven Janas
SENIOR EXECUTIVE VICE PRESIDENT AND
CHIEF OPERATIONS OFFICER: Mary Davis Holt
SENIOR VICE PRESIDENT AND CHIEF FINAN-
CIAL OFFICER: Christopher Hearing

TIME-LIFE BOOKS

PRESIDENT: Joseph A. Kuna
PUBLISHER/MANAGING EDITOR: Neil Kagan
VICE PRESIDENT, NEW PRODUCT
DEVELOPMENT: Amy Golden

What Life Was Like ®
IN EUROPE'S ROMANTIC ERA

EDITOR: Denise Dersin
Deputy Editor: Marion Ferguson Briggs
Art Director: Linda McKnight
Text Editor: Jarelle S. Stein
Associate Editor/Research and Writing:
Sharon Kurtz Thompson
Copyeditor: Leanne Sullivan
Technical Art Specialist: John Drummond
Editorial Assistant: Christine Higgins
Photo Coordinator: David Herod

Special Contributors: Charlotte Anker, Ronald H. Bailey,
Roberta Conlan, Ellen Phillips (chapter text); Jane
Coughran, Stephanie Henke, Jane Martin, Rosanne Scott,
Norma Shaw, Elizabeth Thompson, Lindsay Watkins
(research-writing); Arlene Borden, Cynthia Cather Bur-
ton, Holly Downen, Karen Kinney (research); Constance
Buchanan, Ellen Phillips (editing); Barbara L. Klein
(index and overread)

Correspondents: Christine Hinze (London), Christina
Lieberman (New York), Maria Vincenza Aloisi (Paris);
valuable assistance also provided by Elisabeth Kraemer-
Singh, Angelika Lemmer (Bonn), Trini Bandres (Madrid)

Separations by the Time-Life Imaging Department

NEW PRODUCT DEVELOPMENT:
Director, Elizabeth D. Ward; Project Manager, Barbara M.
Sheppard; Director of Marketing, Mary Ann Donaghy;
Marketing Manager, Paul Fontaine; Associate Marketing
Manager, Erin Gaskins

MARKETING: Director, Pamela R. Farrell; Marketing
Manager, Nancy Gallo; Associate Marketing Manager,
Erin Trefry

Senior Vice President, Law & Business Affairs:
Randolph H. Elkins
Vice President, Finance: Claudia Goldberg
Vice President, Book Production: Patricia Pascale
Vice President, Imaging: Marjann Caldwell
Director, Publishing Technology: Betsi McGrath
Director, Editorial Administration: Barbara Levitt
Director, Photography and Research: John Conrad Weiser
Director, Quality Assurance: James King
Manager, Technical Services: Anne Topp
Senior Production Manager: Ken Sabol
Manager, Copyedit/Page Makeup: Debby Tait
Production Manager: Virginia Reardon
Chief Librarian: Louise D. Forstall

Consultant:

Arthur Herman currently is Visiting Associate Professor of
History at George Mason University and Coordinator of
the Western Heritage Program at the Smithsonian Institution in Washington, D.C. He completed his Ph.D. at Johns
Hopkins University, where his dissertation won the prestigious Brittingham Prize. Dr. Herman's book, *The Idea of
Decline in Western History,* was published in 1997 and has
since been translated into German, Spanish, and Por-
tuguese. He also has published numerous articles in periodicals such as *The Journal of Modern History* and *Cahiers
du Dix-Septième.*

Library of Congress Cataloging-in-Publication Data
What life was like in Europe's Romantic Era : Europe,
1789-1848 / by the editors of Time-Life Books,
Alexandria, Virginia.
          p. cm. — (What life was like ; 17)
          Includes bibliographical references and index.
          ISBN 0-7835-5466-4
          1. Europe—Social life and customs—18th century.
2. Europe—Social life and customs—19th century. I. Title:
In Europe's Romantic Era. II. Time-Life Books. III. What
life was like series ; 17.
D299 .W46 2000   99-055226
940.2'7—dc21

10 9 8 7 6 5 4 3 2 1